Hamilton Troll's
Coloring & Activity
BOOK

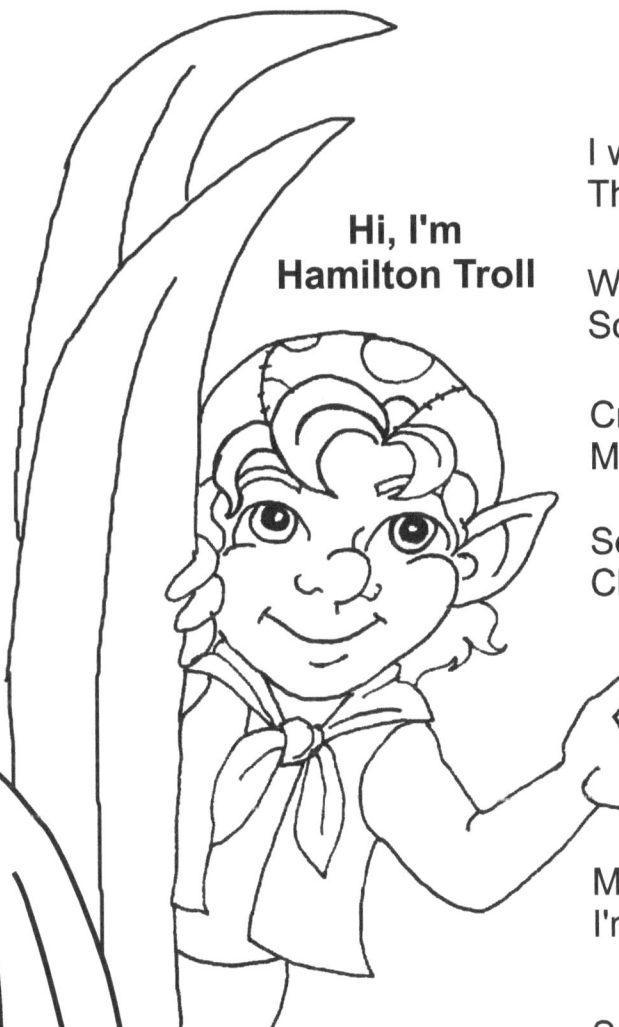

**Hi, I'm
Hamilton Troll**

I wanted to ask, if you'll be my friend.
Throughout this book, 'till the very end.

We can color together. Won't that be fun?
So much to do until we're done.

Crossword puzzles, games and then,
More coloring pages to do again.

Secret messages to you.
Clap your hands, so much to do!

I hope you enjoy
this book of mine.
Then when you're done
you can go online.

My website has games and more to do.
I'm always thinking of things for you.

So explore my world, every girl and boy.
It's a troll's life. Go on, enjoy!

www.HamiltonTroll.com

Hamilton Troll's Coloring & Activity Book

Manufactured in the United States of America.

ISBN-13: 978-1-941345-05-4 Paperback

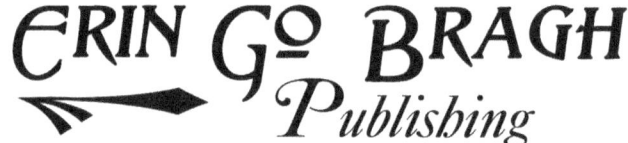

Mazes, Word Games & Designs by Kathleen J. Shields
Character Illustrations by Leigh A. Klug

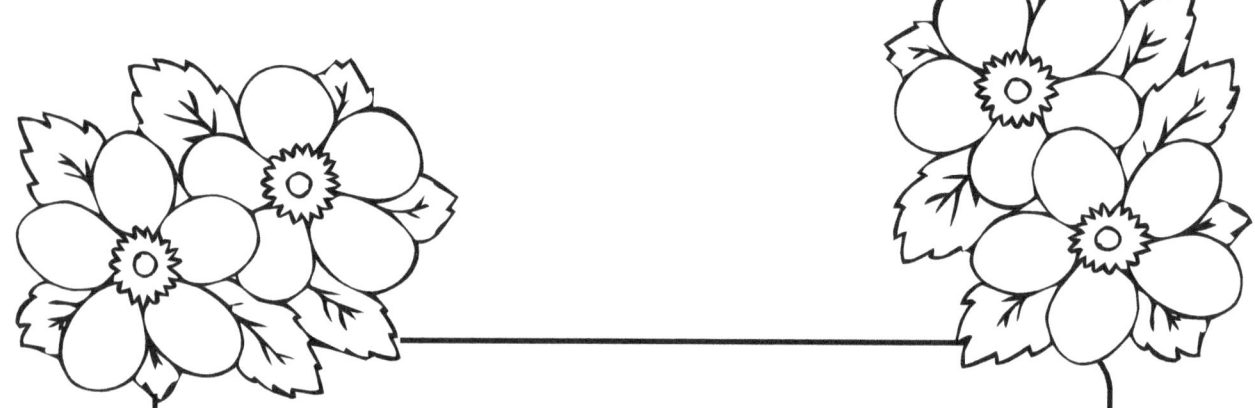

THIS BOOK BELONGS TO:

To receive updates or additional information, please visit our website:

www.HamiltonTroll.com

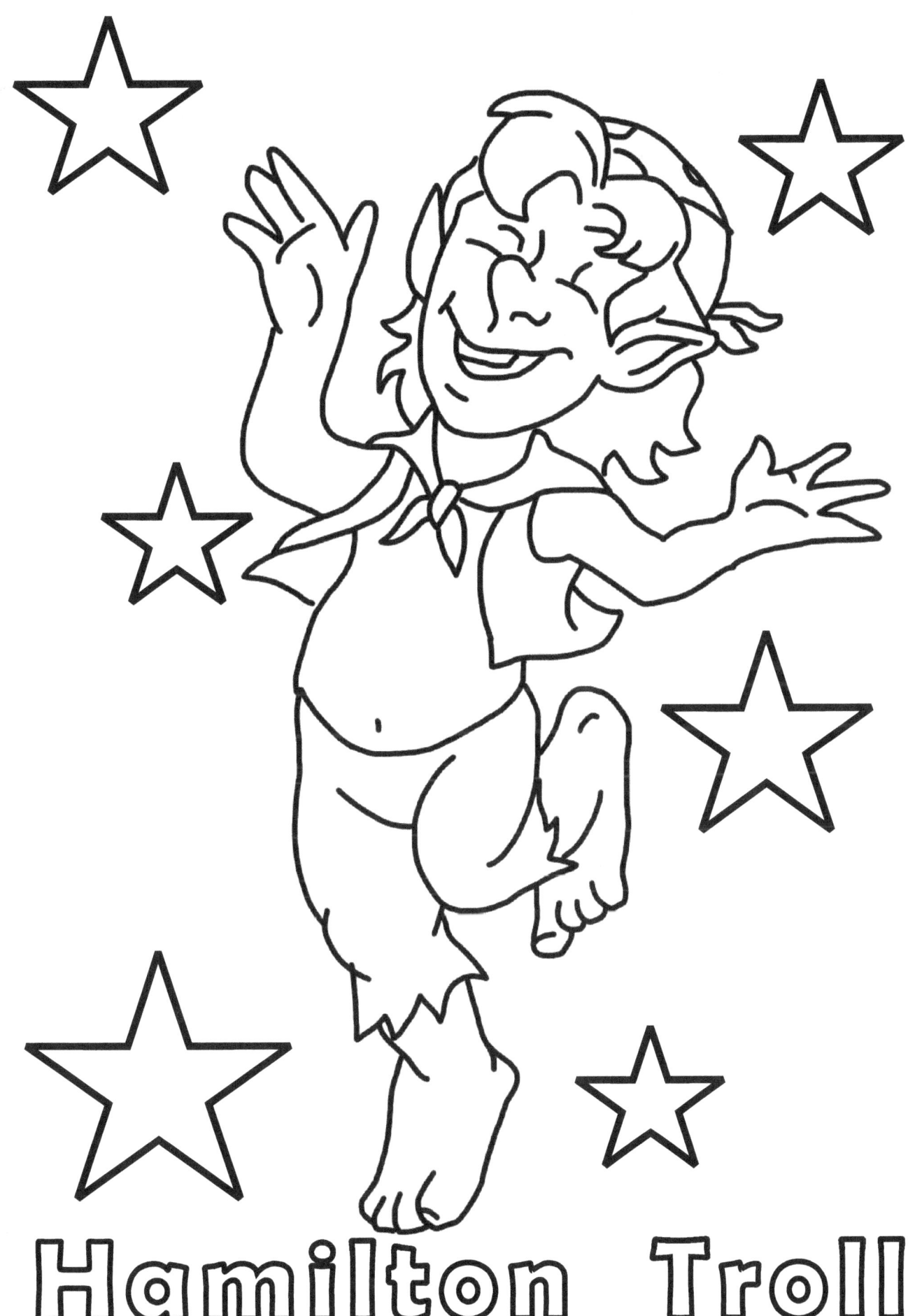

Hamilton Troll

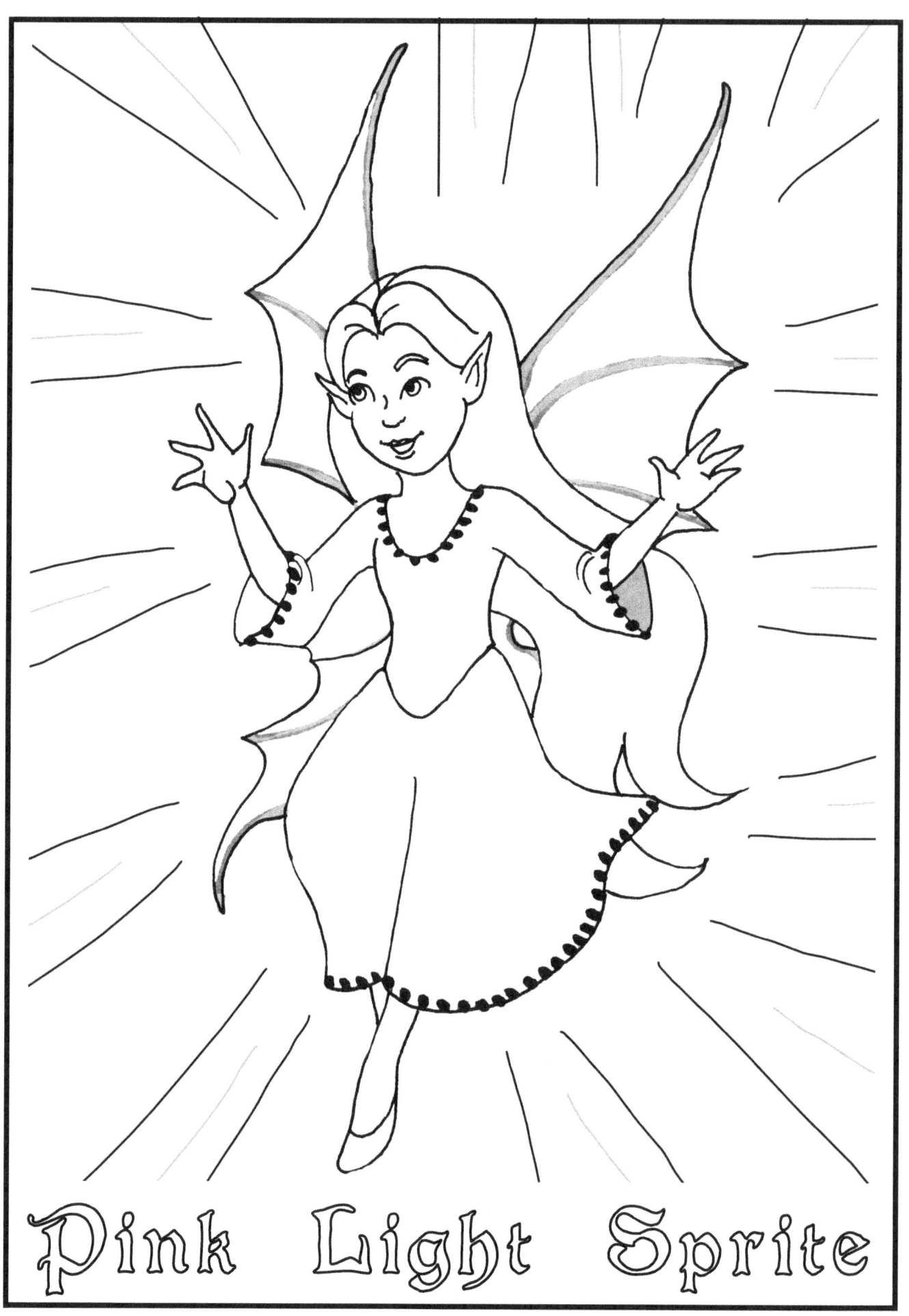

Pink Light Sprite

Help Hamilton Troll find Pink Light Sprite

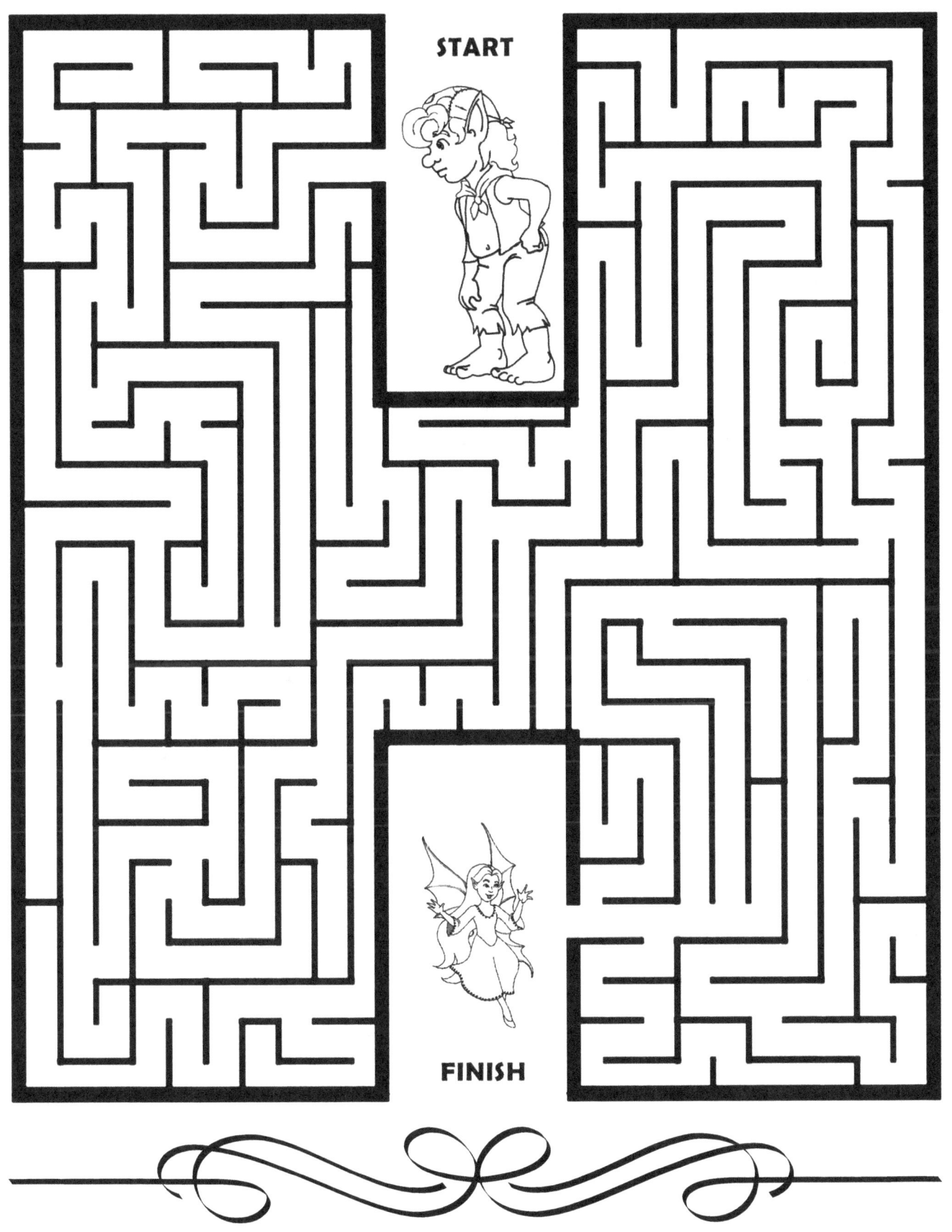

START

FINISH

COLOR BY NUMBERS

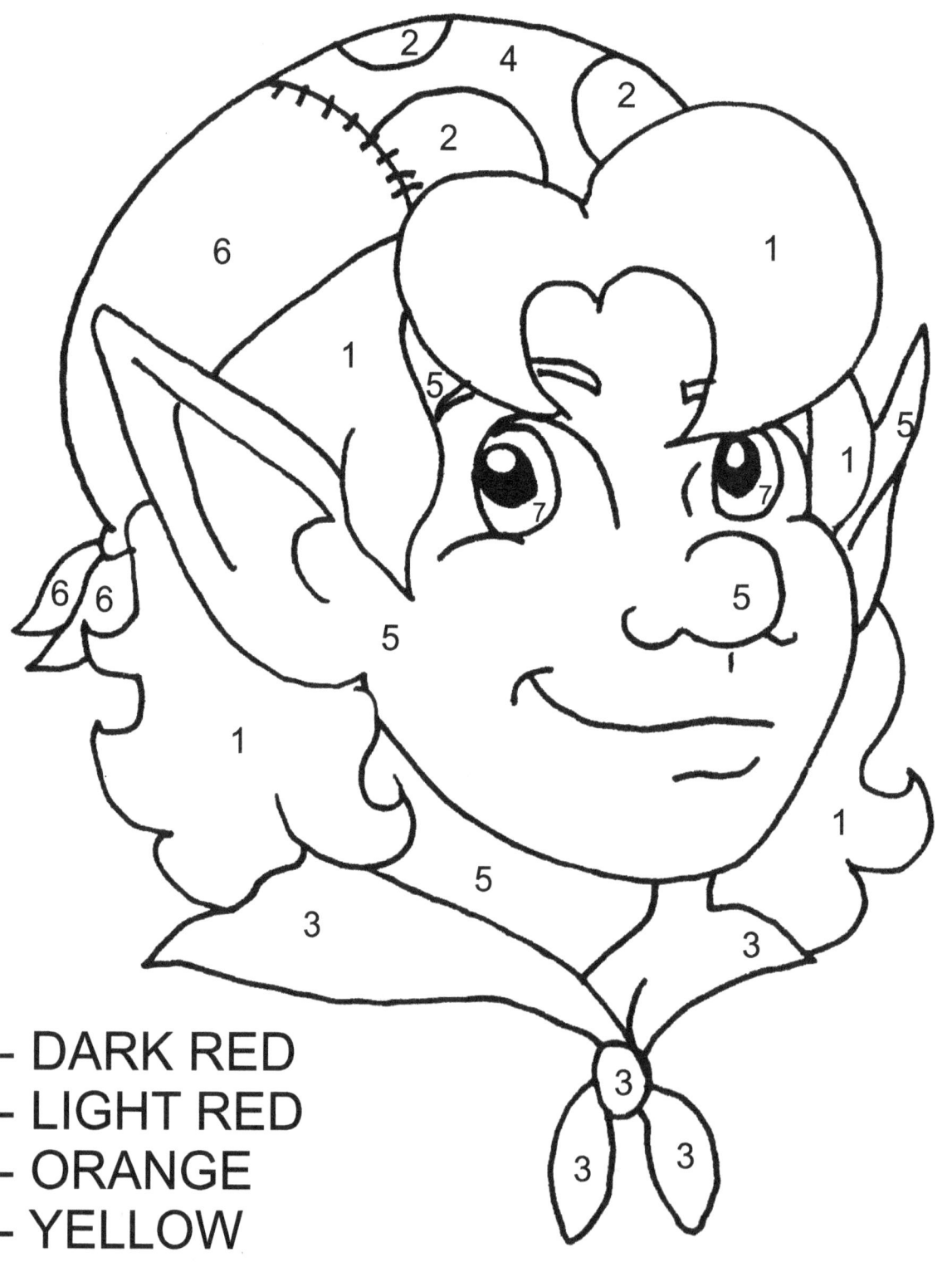

1 - DARK RED
2 - LIGHT RED
3 - ORANGE
4 - YELLOW
5 - LIGHT GREEN
6 - DARK GREEN
7 - BROWN

Fill in the areas with the color of the number.

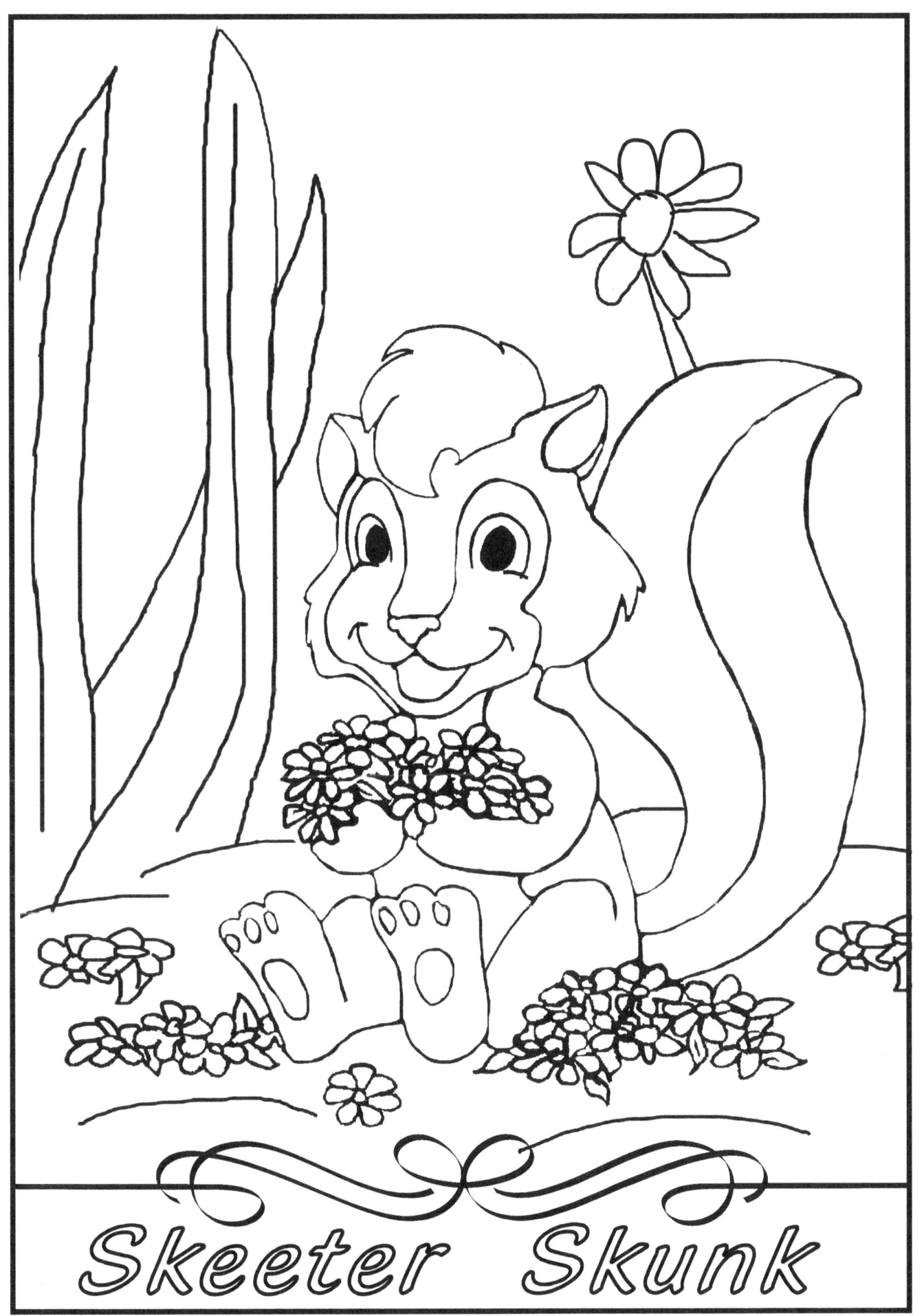

Skeeter Skunk

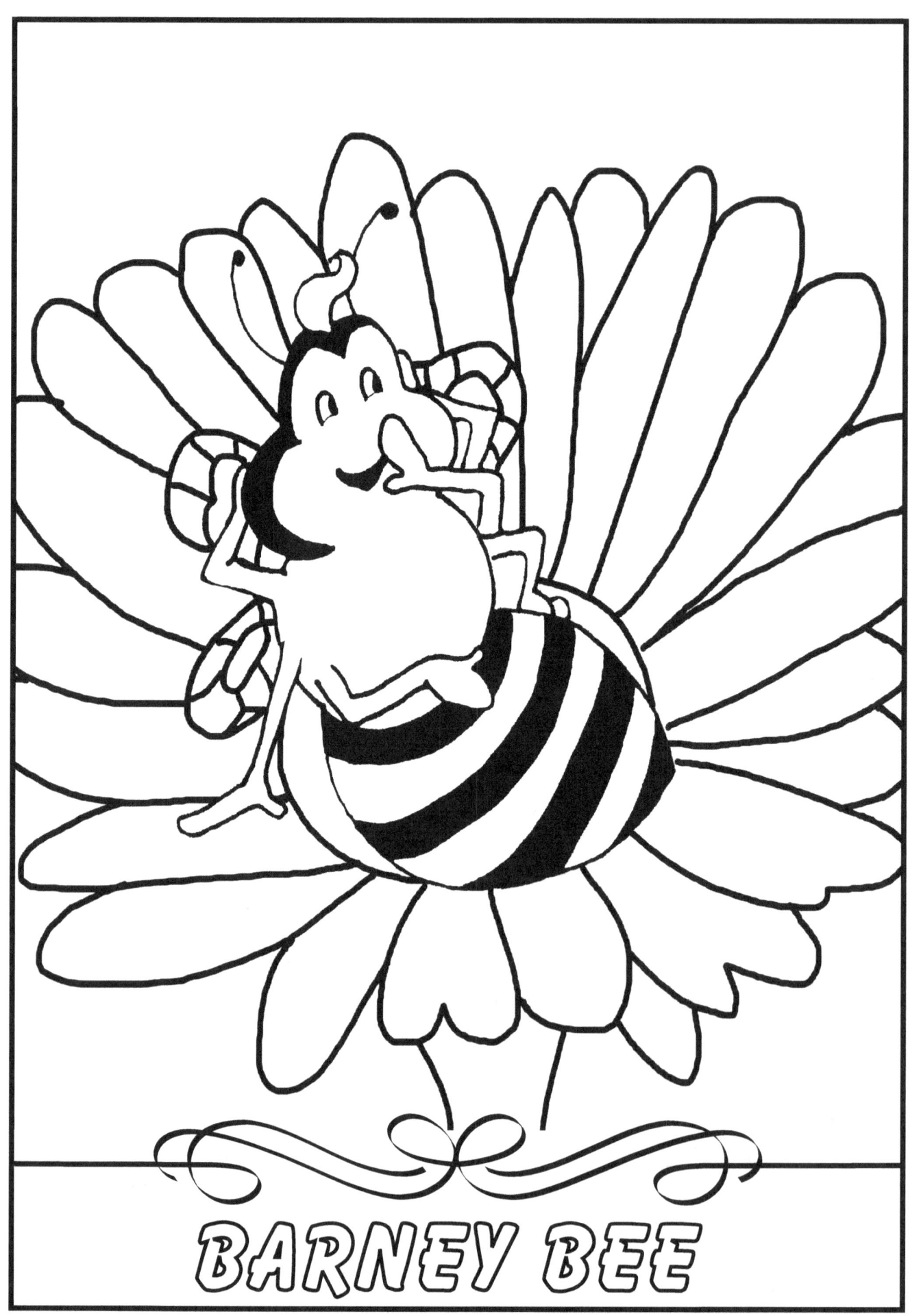

BARNEY BEE

DID YOU KNOW?
BUMBLE BEES

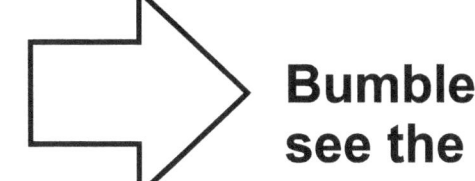

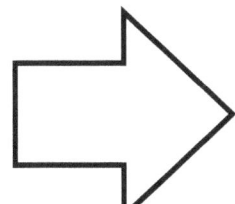 Bumble Bees are color blind. They can't see the color RED.

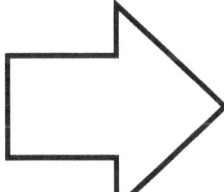 Male drone bumble bees can't sting.

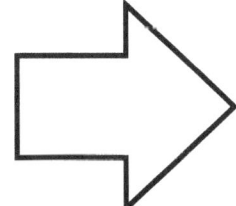 Some Bumble bee's don't live in hives, most live in the ground.

They only make enough honey to feed themselves.

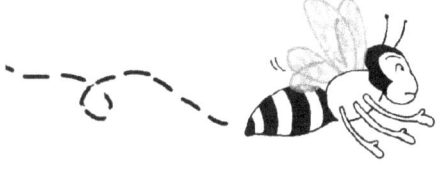

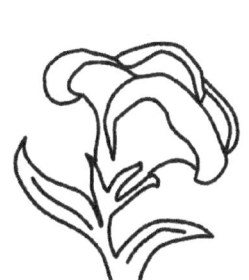

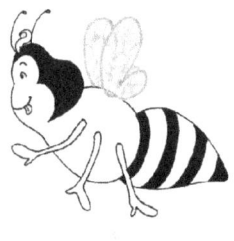

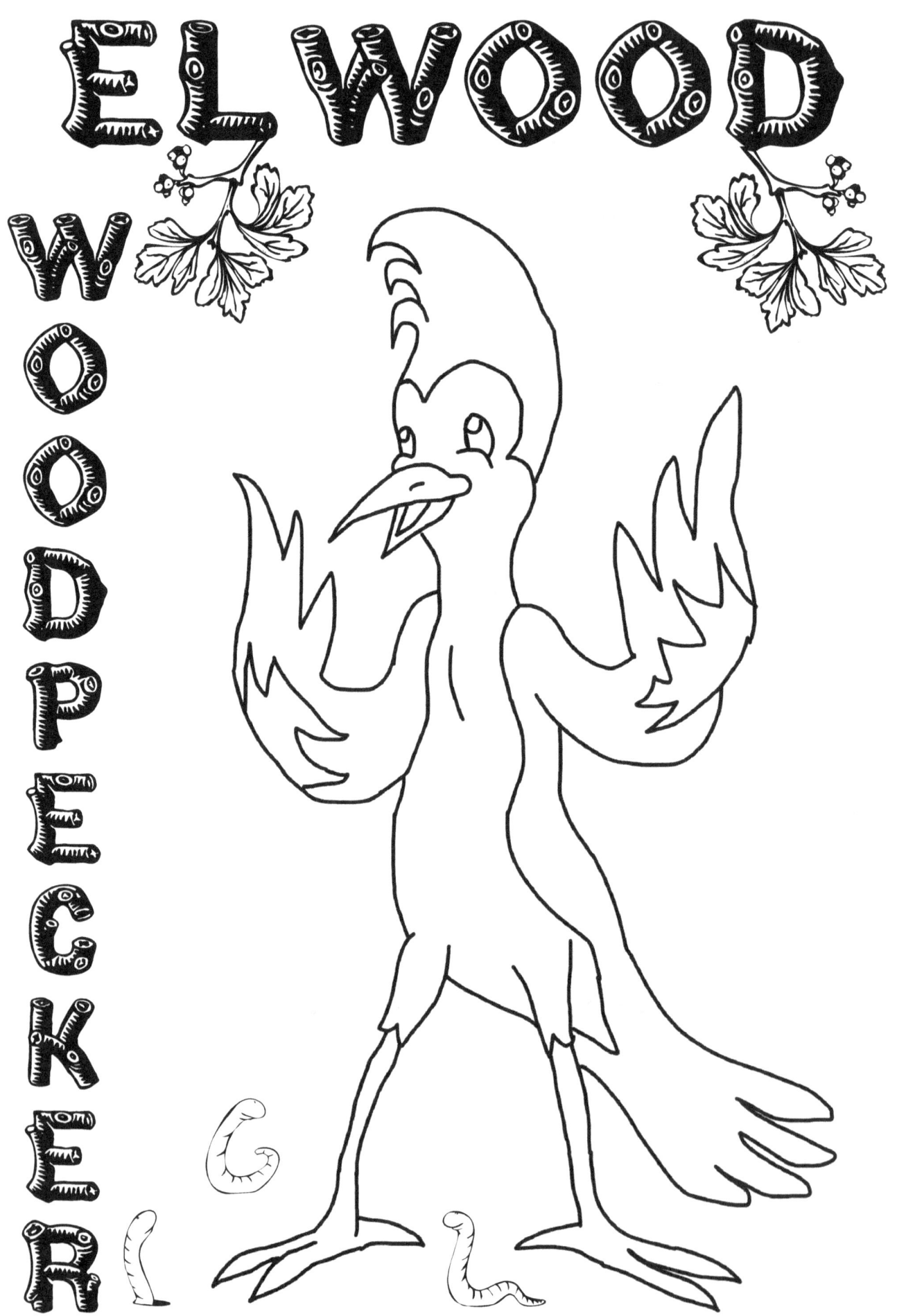

DID YOU KNOW?

WOODPECKERS

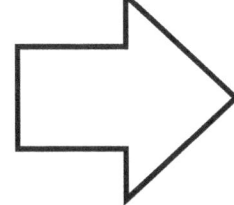 Woodpeckers tap holes in wood and trees, in hopes of finding bugs to eat but they also drink tree sap and eat fruits, nuts and seeds.

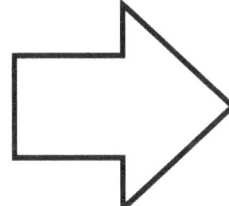 Woodpecker feet have toes that face front AND back so they can grip hold of anything (tree or pole).

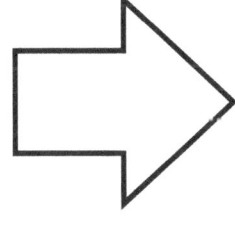 Woodpeckers don't sing but they are really good drummers! They communicate by tapping (on anything) so if you ever see a woodpecker drumming on something like a metal pole or trash can, they're not trying to find food, but trying to talk to another woodpecker.

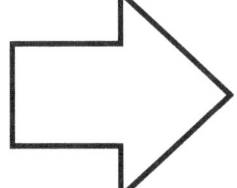 Woodpeckers can peck up to 20 times per second!

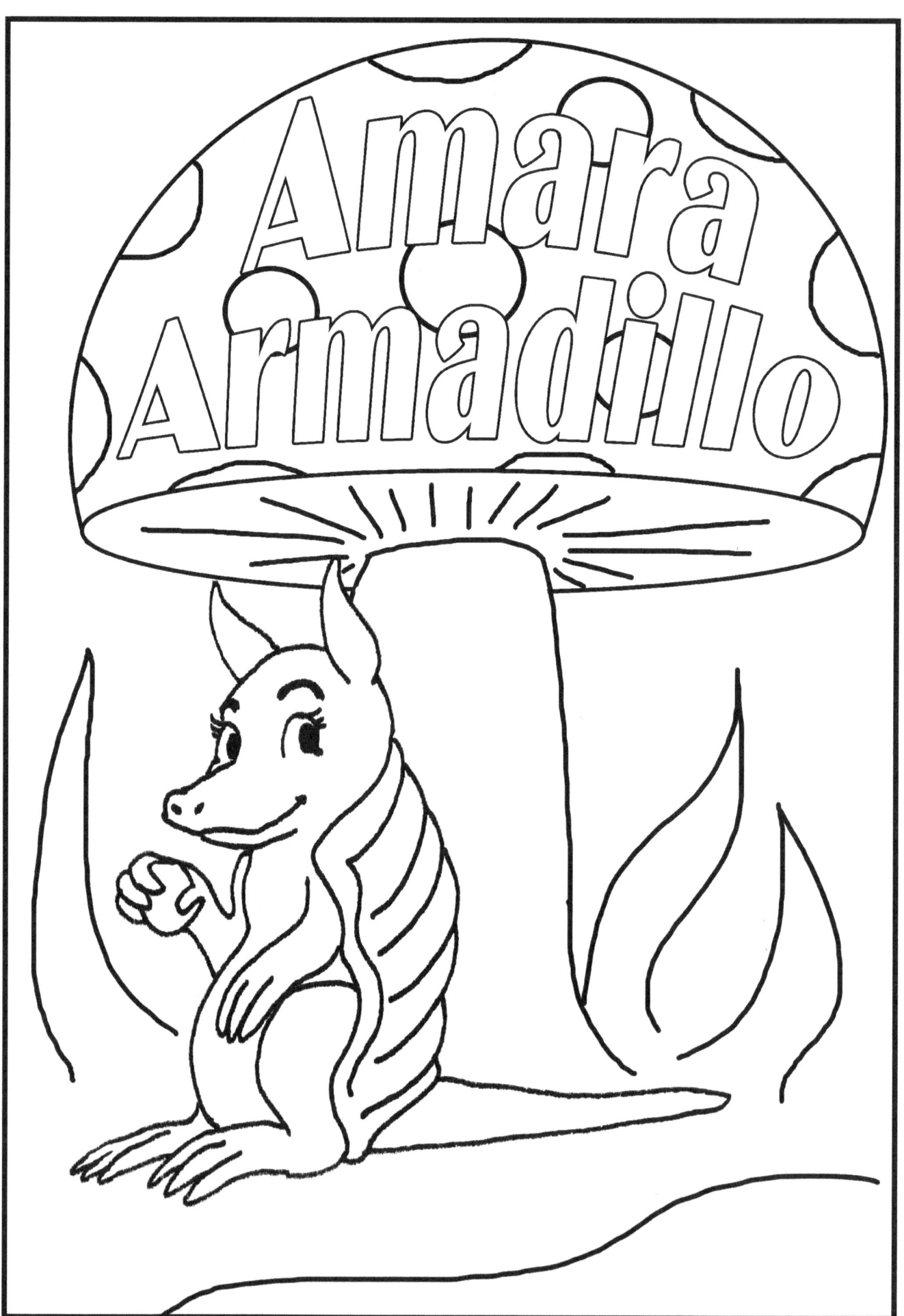

DID YOU KNOW?
ARMADILLOs

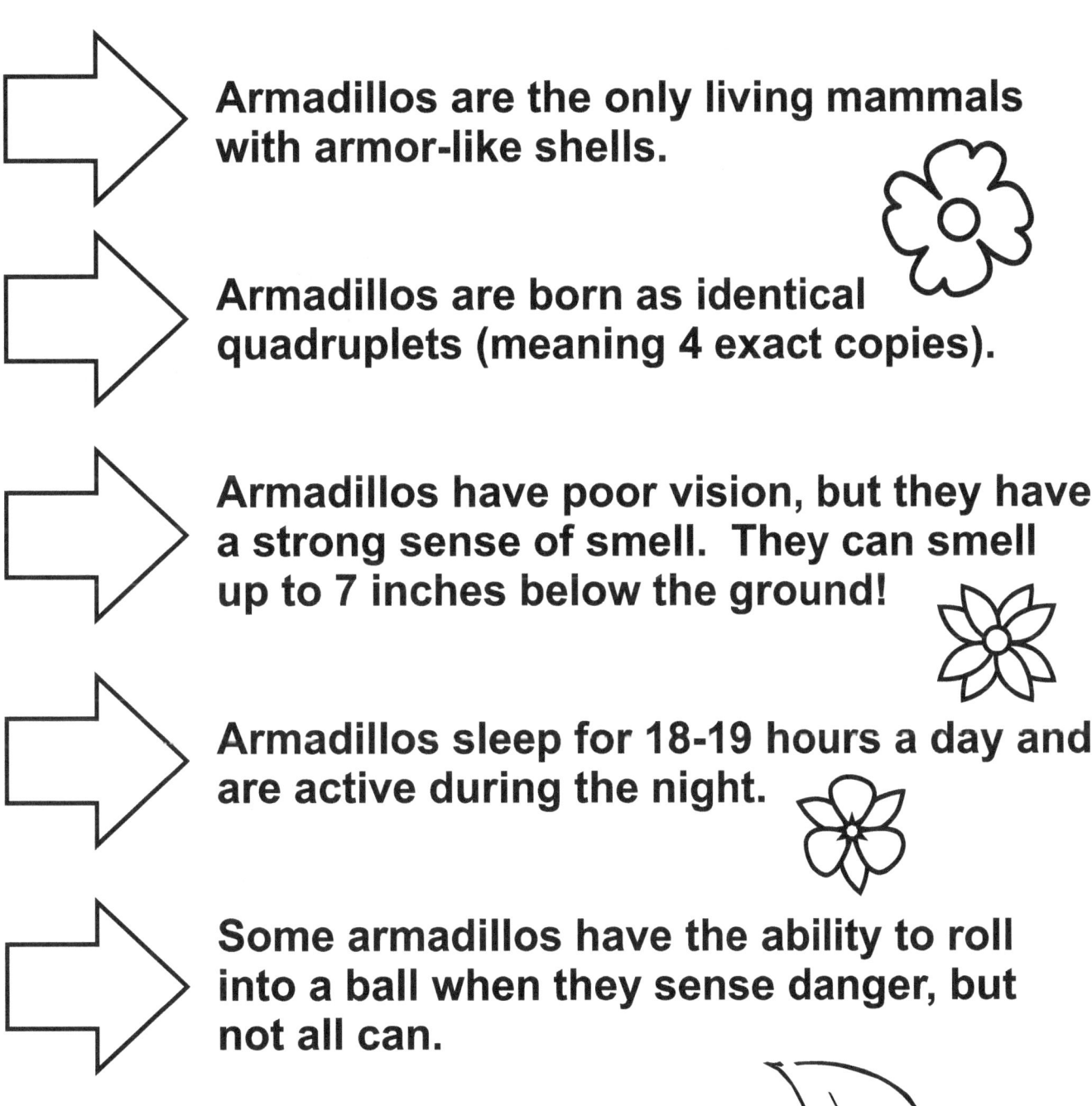

➡ Armadillos are the only living mammals with armor-like shells.

➡ Armadillos are born as identical quadruplets (meaning 4 exact copies).

➡ Armadillos have poor vision, but they have a strong sense of smell. They can smell up to 7 inches below the ground!

➡ Armadillos sleep for 18-19 hours a day and are active during the night.

➡ Some armadillos have the ability to roll into a ball when they sense danger, but not all can.

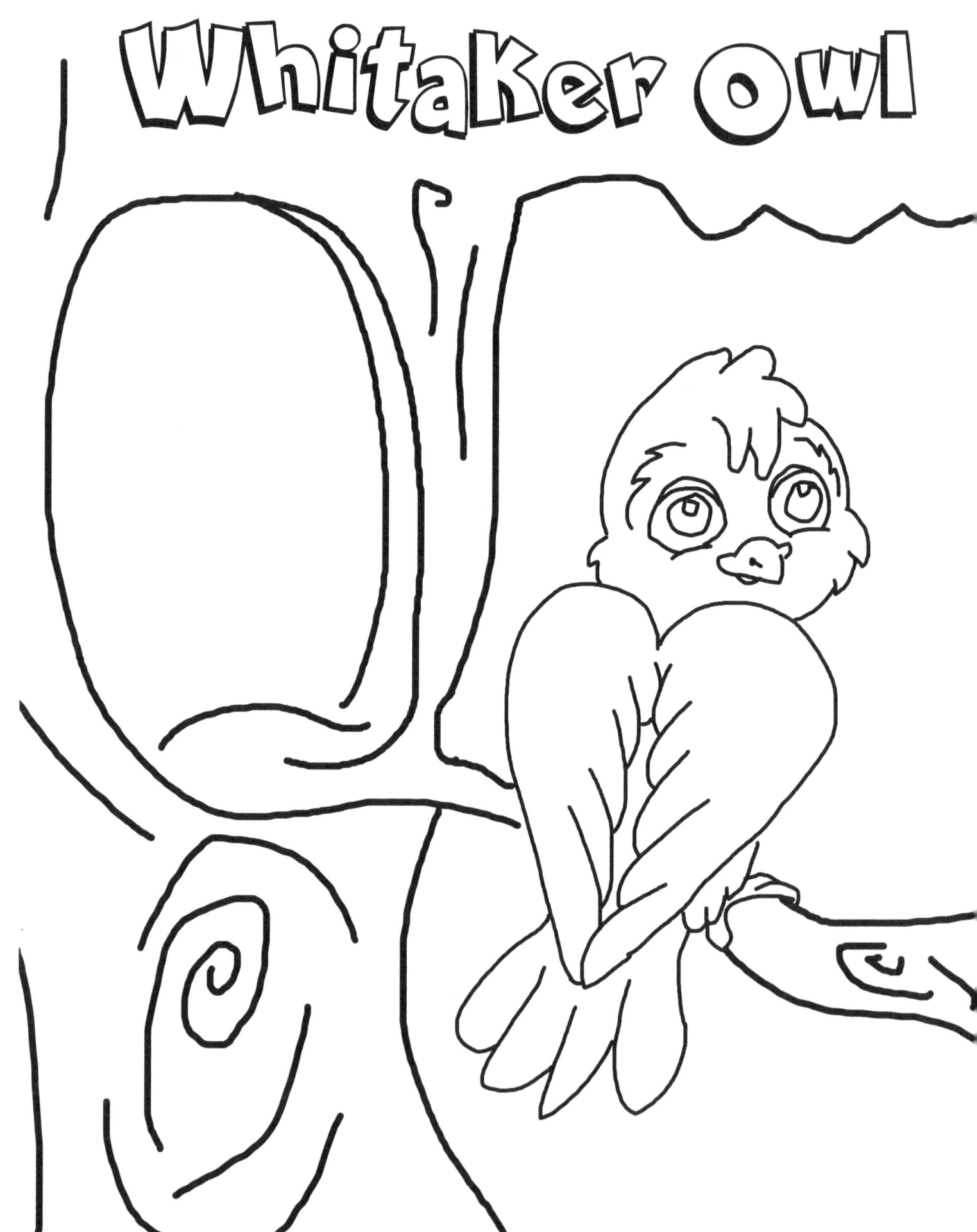

DID YOU KNOW?
OWLS

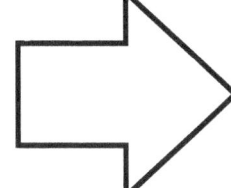 **Owls cannot chew their food because they do not have teeth. Instead, they swallow their food whole.**

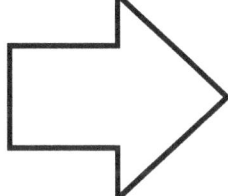 **When their food contains things they can't digest, they regurgitate pellets (throw-up).**

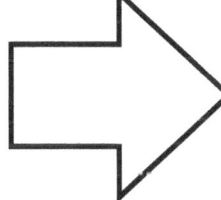 **Owls are unable to move their eyes which means they must turn their entire head to see in a different direction.**

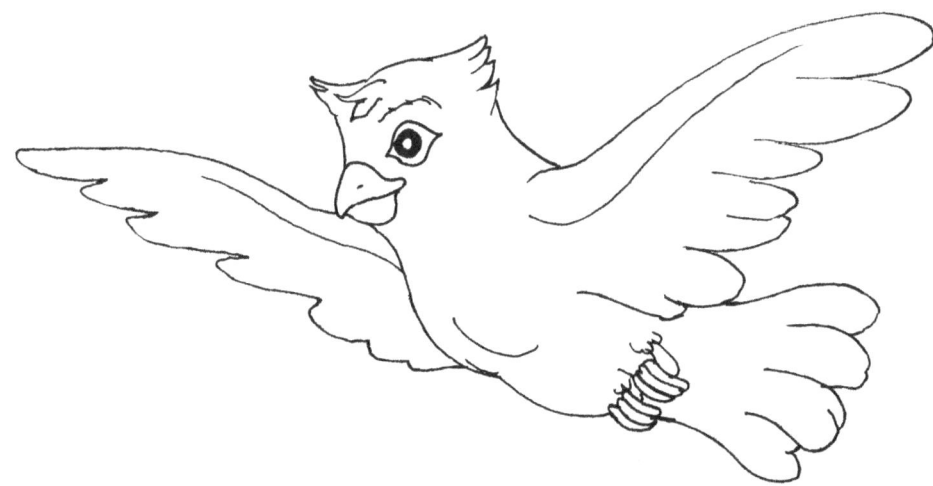

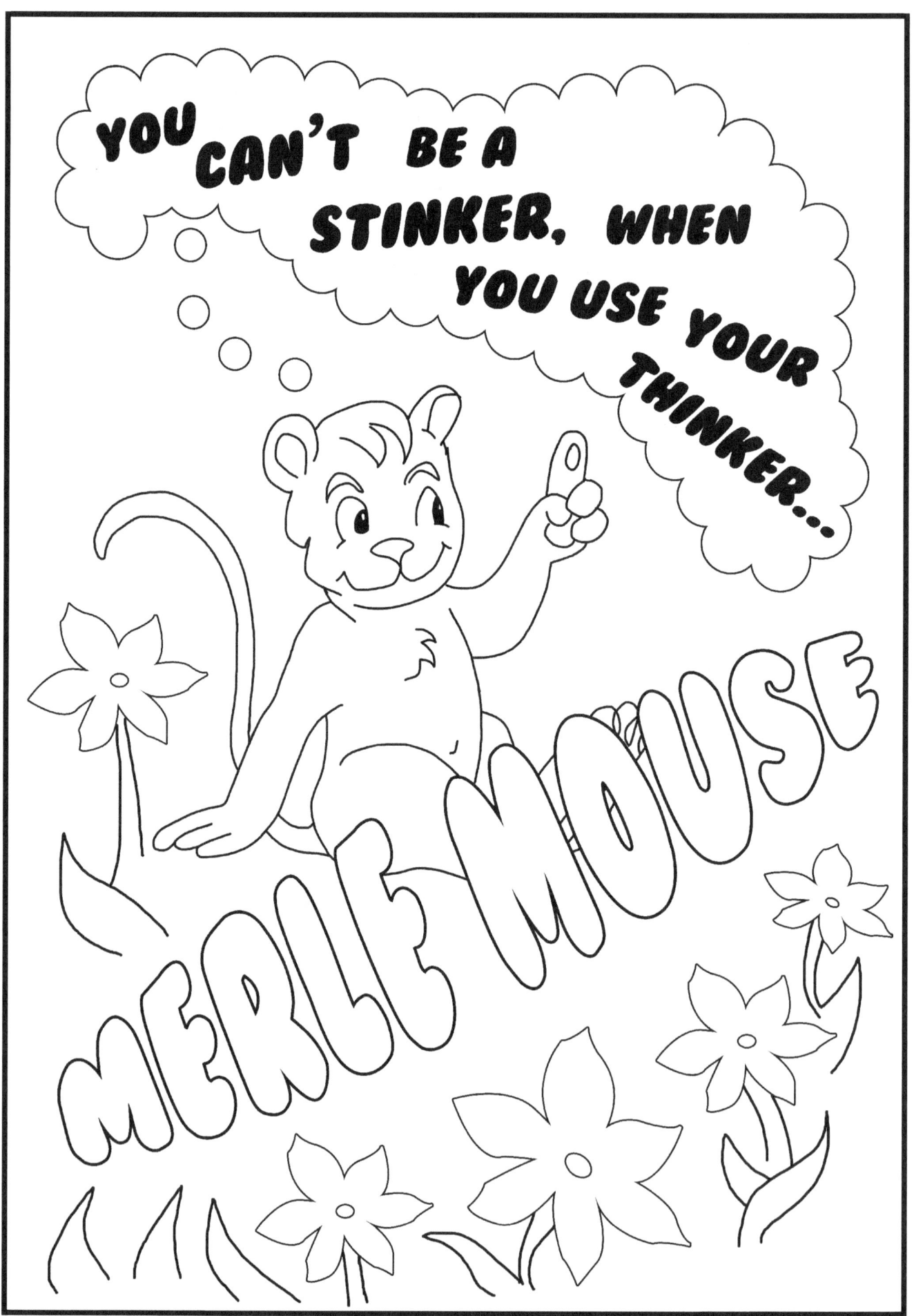

What Does Hamilton Troll Dream About?

Draw your idea in the bubble below.

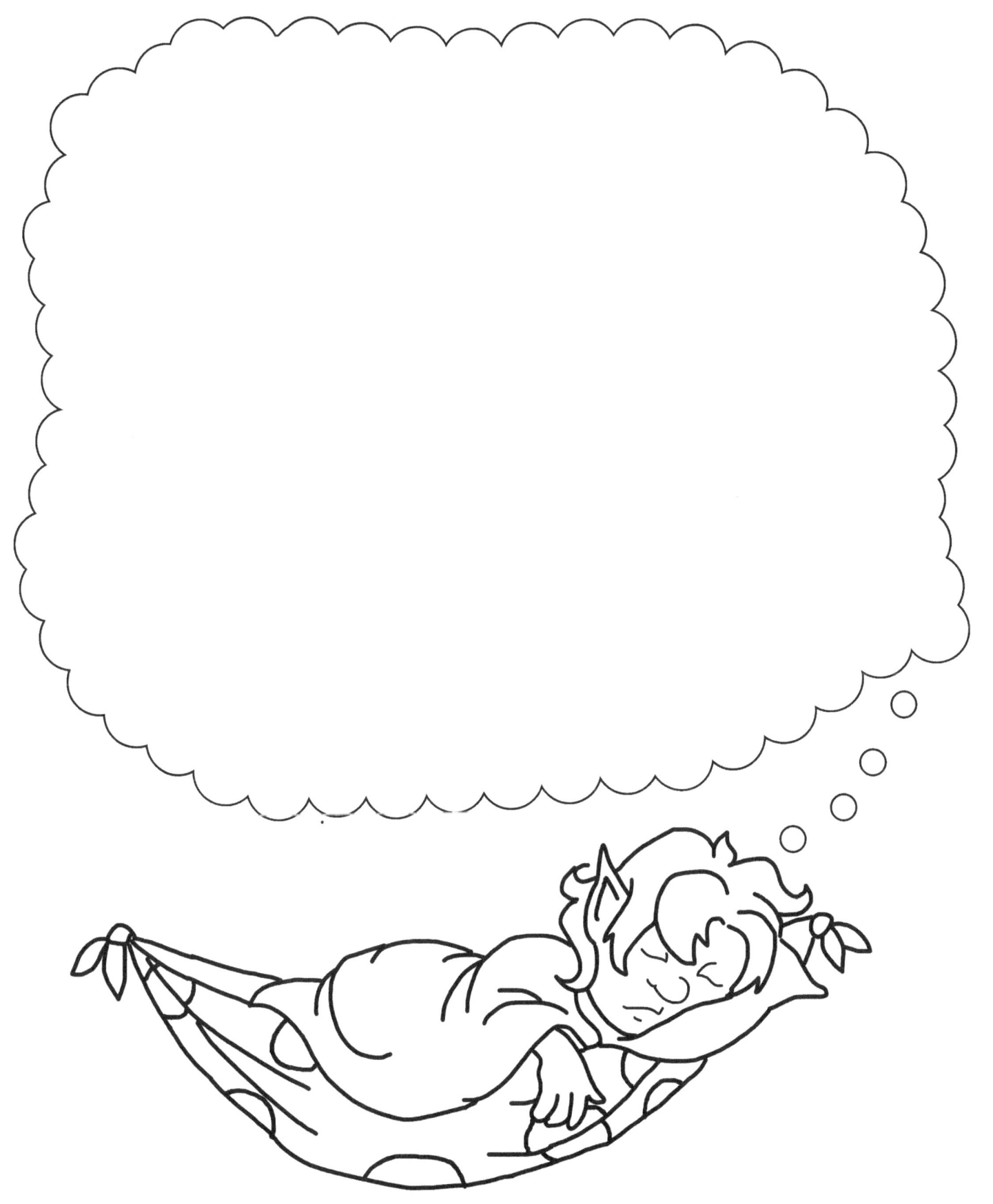

Trolls are usually hard to find.

But in this word search they are very easy.
How many times can you find the
word TROLL in this search?

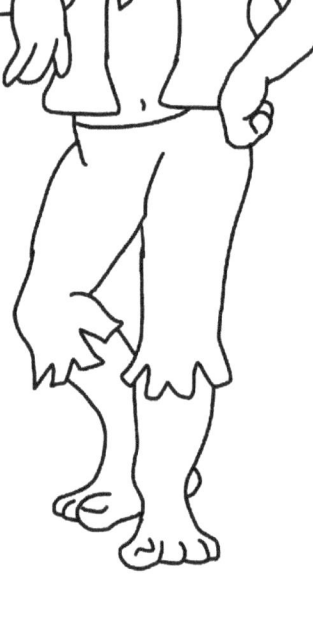

T	R	O	L	L	O	R	T	R	L
R	R	T	R	O	L	L	R	L	L
O	T	O	L	L	R	R	O	T	O
L	L	O	R	T	T	O	L	L	R
L	L	O	R	L	R	O	L	T	T
R	L	T	O	L	L	O	T	R	O
T	R	O	L	O	L	L	O	R	T
R	L	R	R	R	O	L	T	L	O
O	L	L	O	T	L	L	O	O	L
L	O	L	T	L	L	O	R	T	R
L	R	O	R	O	R	R	O	R	O
R	T	R	R	O	T	T	L	R	L
O	R	T	R	O	L	L	O	R	T

How many
times did
you find
the word
TROLL?

_____

Pink Light Sprite

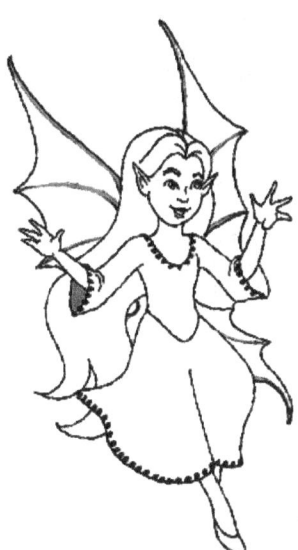

will always be around but will be out of sight...
which makes her hard to find. But in this word
search you can find the word SPRITE a whole
lot of times!

How many times can you find SPRITE?

E	T	I	R	P	S	P	R	I	T	E
E	S	T	S	P	R	I	T	E	S	R
S	S	P	R	I	T	E	S	R	S	P
E	T	I	R	P	S	S	P	R	P	S
E	T	I	R	P	S	P	R	S	R	E
E	S	P	R	I	E	I	I	S	I	T
T	T	S	P	R	T	E	T	R	T	I
I	S	I	T	E	I	R	E	P	E	R
R	P	S	R	S	R	R	I	T	E	P
P	R	I	T	P	P	T	R	I	P	S
S	P	R	I	T	S	S	P	R	I	T	E
P	R	I	S	P	R	I	T	E	T	R

HELP BARNEY BEE FIND HIS WAY THROUGH THE FLOWER

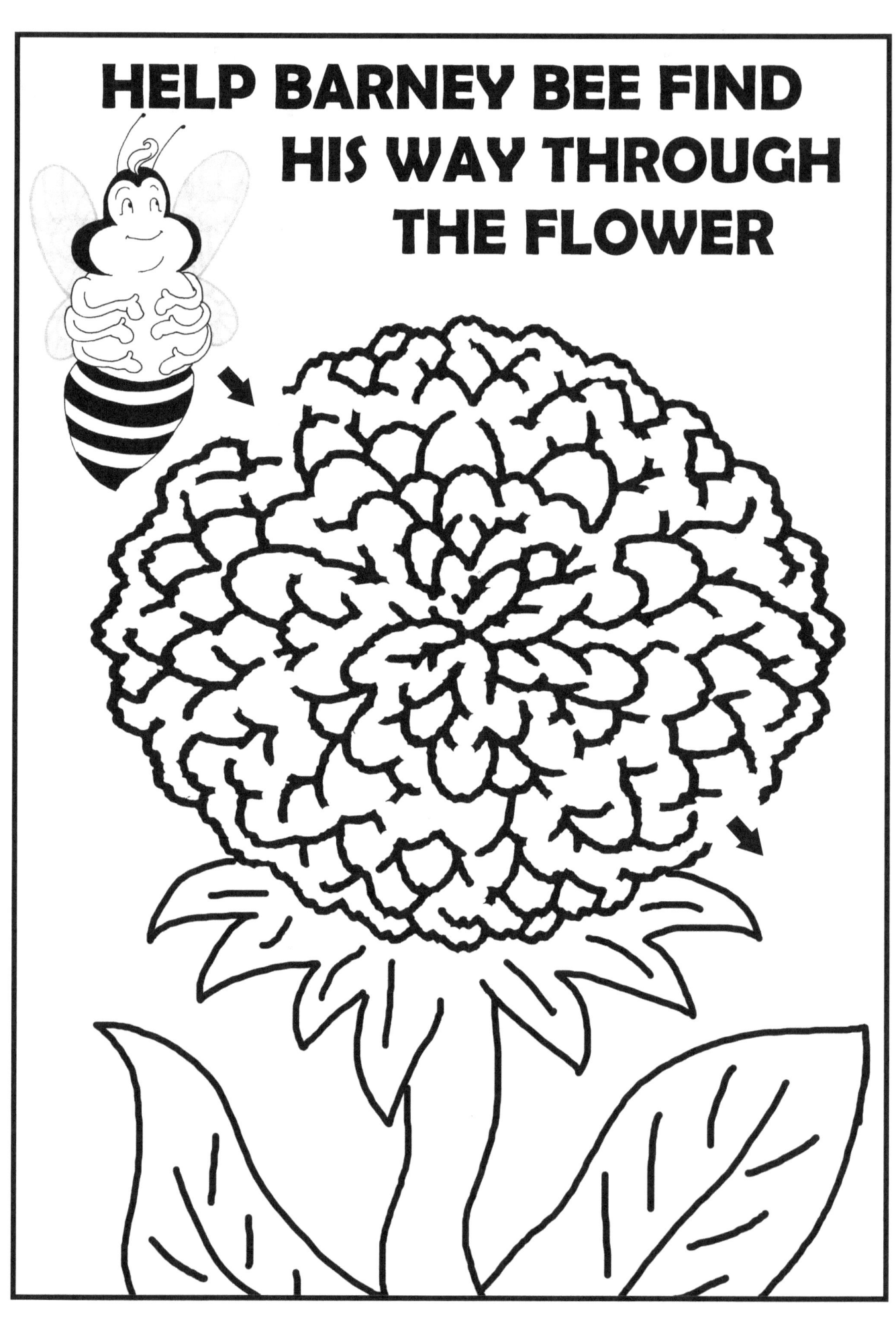

LITTLE BUNNY

"When I eat these red berries, I become a real stinker."

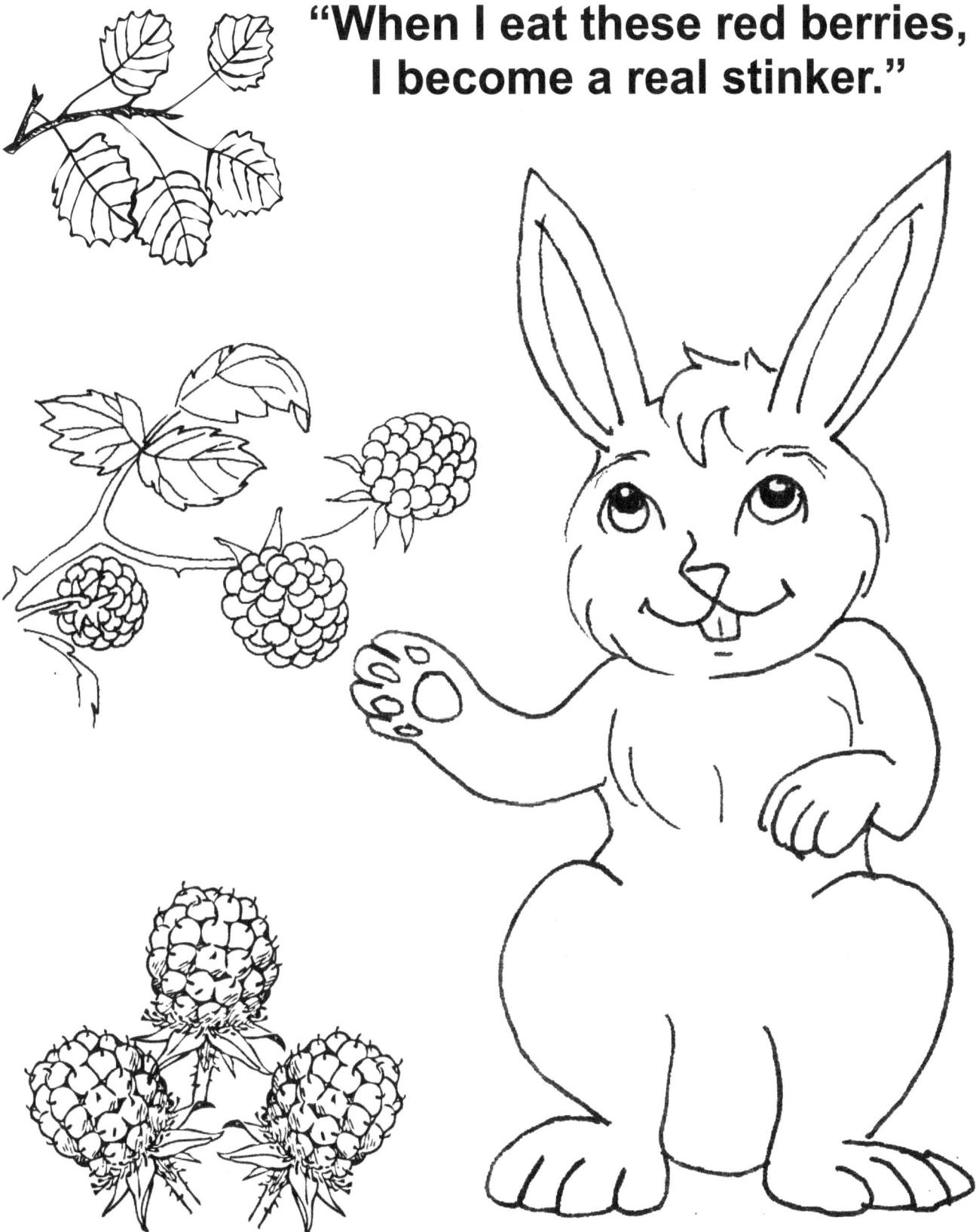

THE BEAVER

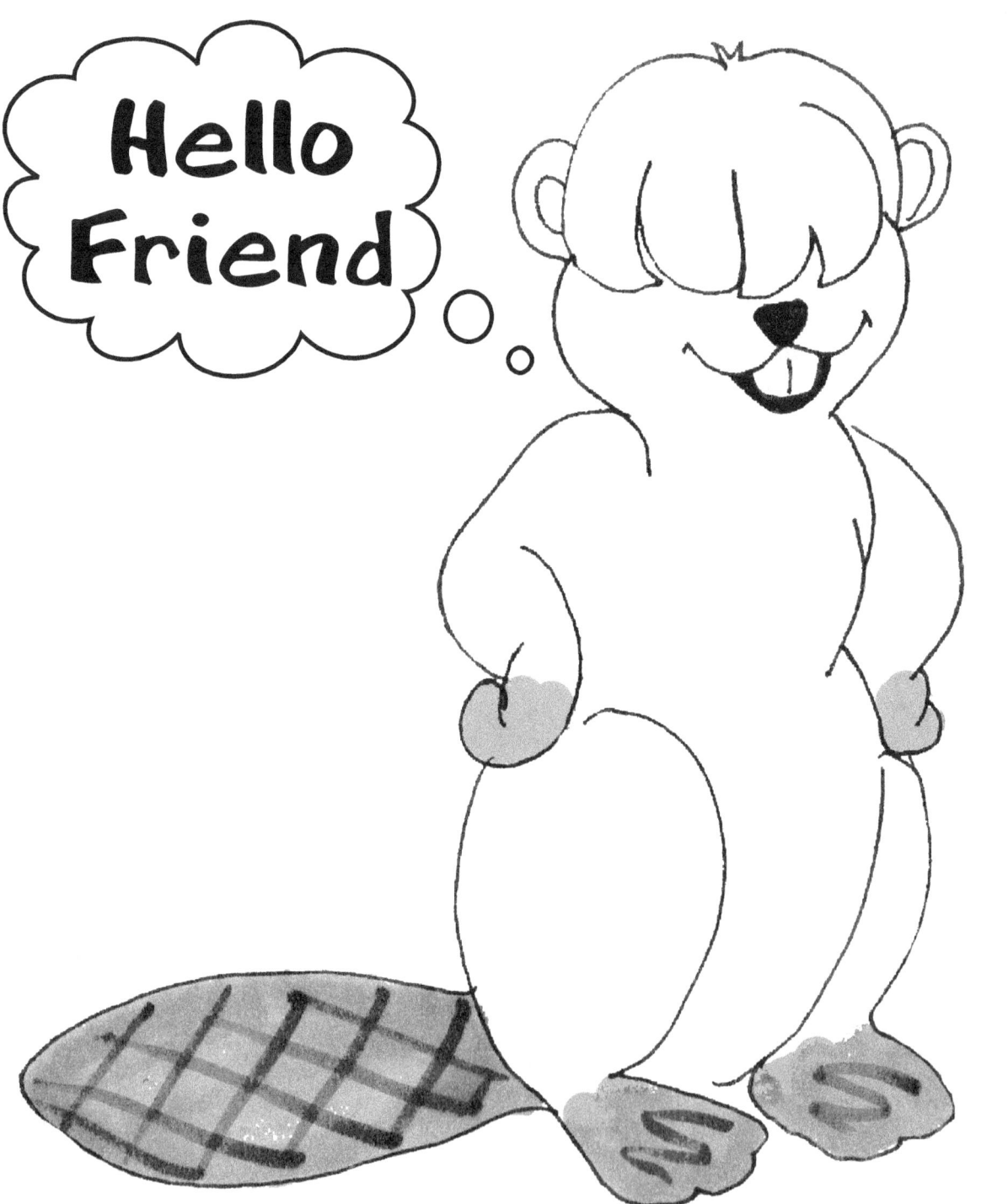

BAXTER

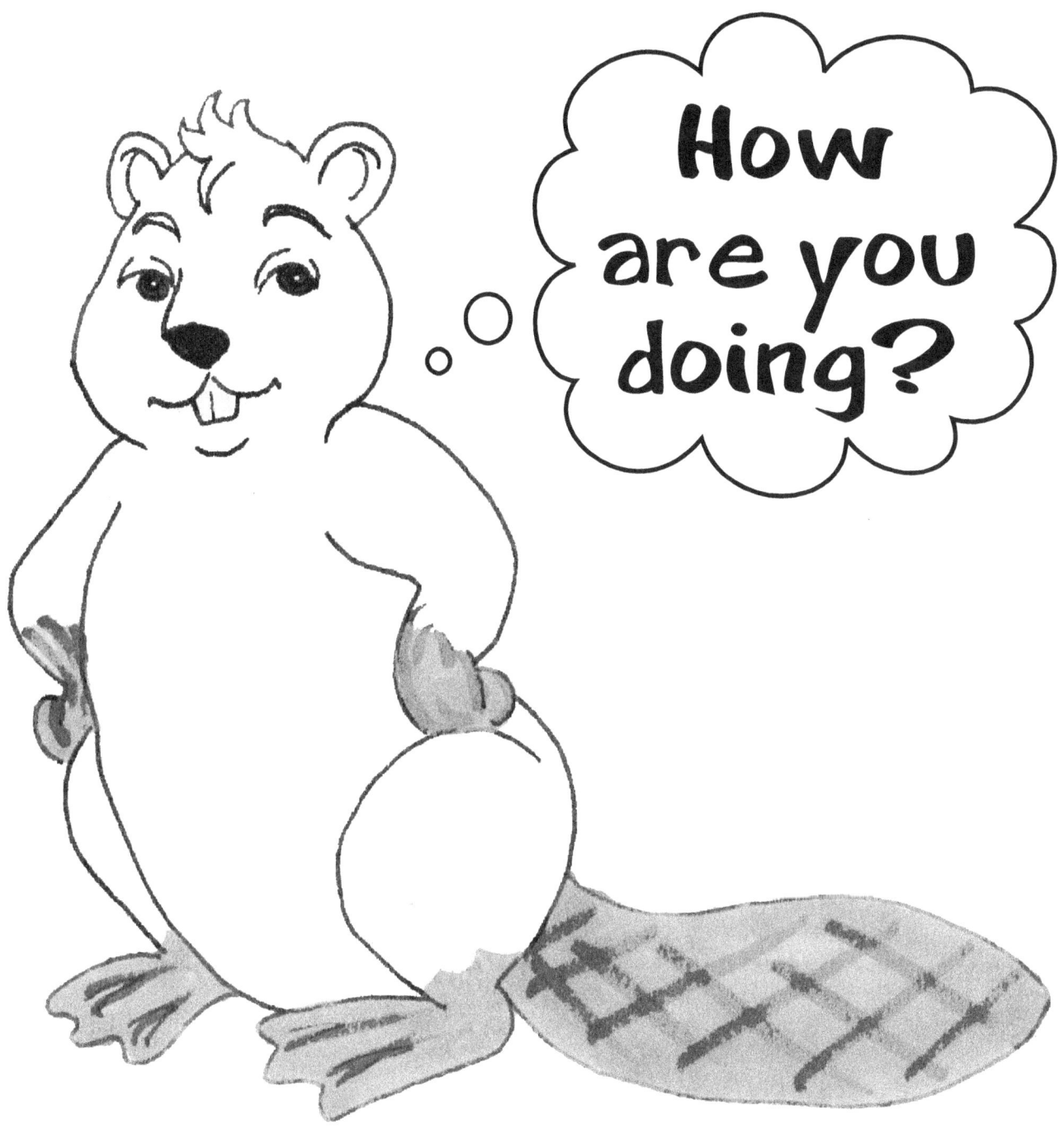

DID YOU KNOW?
BEAVERS

A beaver is semi-aquatic, meaning they live in the water but can walk on land.

Beavers have thick fur and webbed feet (like a duck) for swimming.

Beavers have large flat tails they use as paddles and for packing mud on the dams.

Beavers have sharp teeth for gnawing on wood, that grow back like fingernails.

Beavers are herbivores, they eat wood and plants; like water lilies.

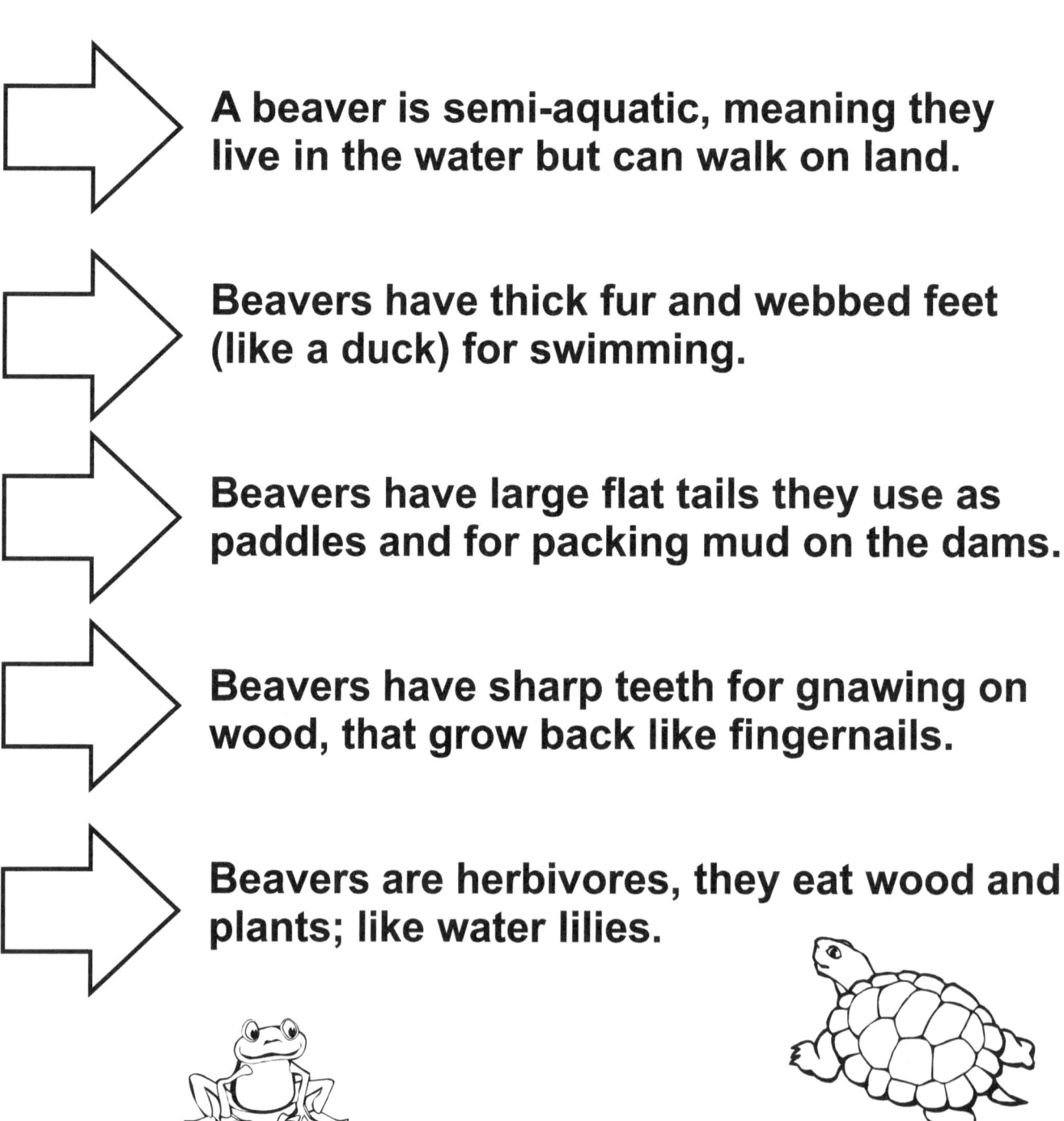

DID YOU KNOW?
BEAVER DAMS

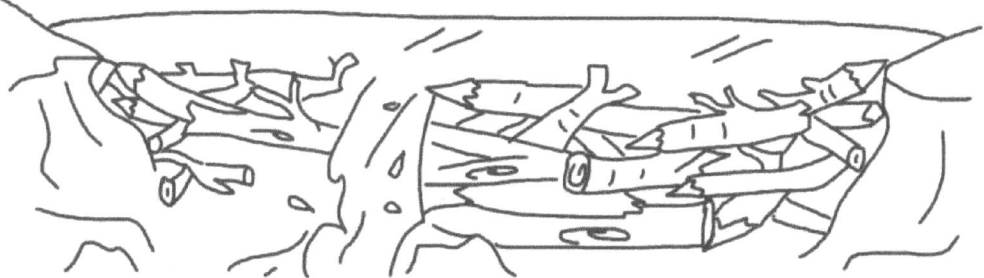

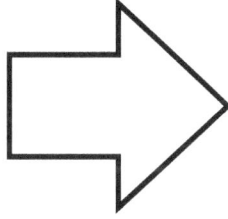 There is a theory that beavers build dams to silence the rushing water sound, which makes their homes quieter but also provides the ability to hear any approaching predators so they can dive below the water for protection.

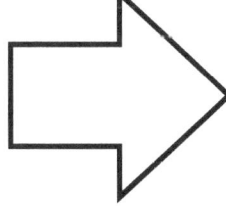 Beaver dams have a profound effect on ecosystems, by creating wetlands; lush environments which attract fish, ducks, frogs and other creatures.

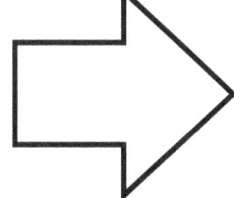 The largest beaver dam was over 2,780 feet long (850 meters) in Wood Buffalo National Park in Alberta, Canada.

BEAVER DAMS

The primary reason that beavers build dams is to create a safe place where they can build their homes. These homes called lodges are built in deep, still pools of water and have underwater entryways.

There are typically two dens within the lodge, one for drying off after exiting the water, and another, drier one, where the family actually lives.

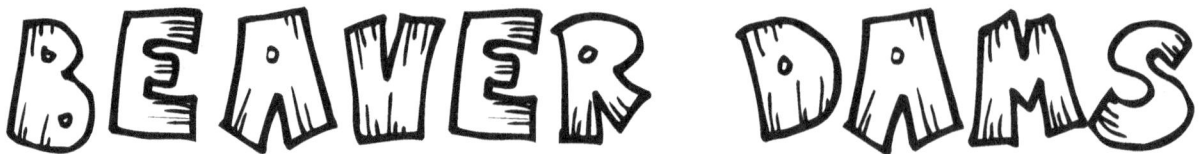

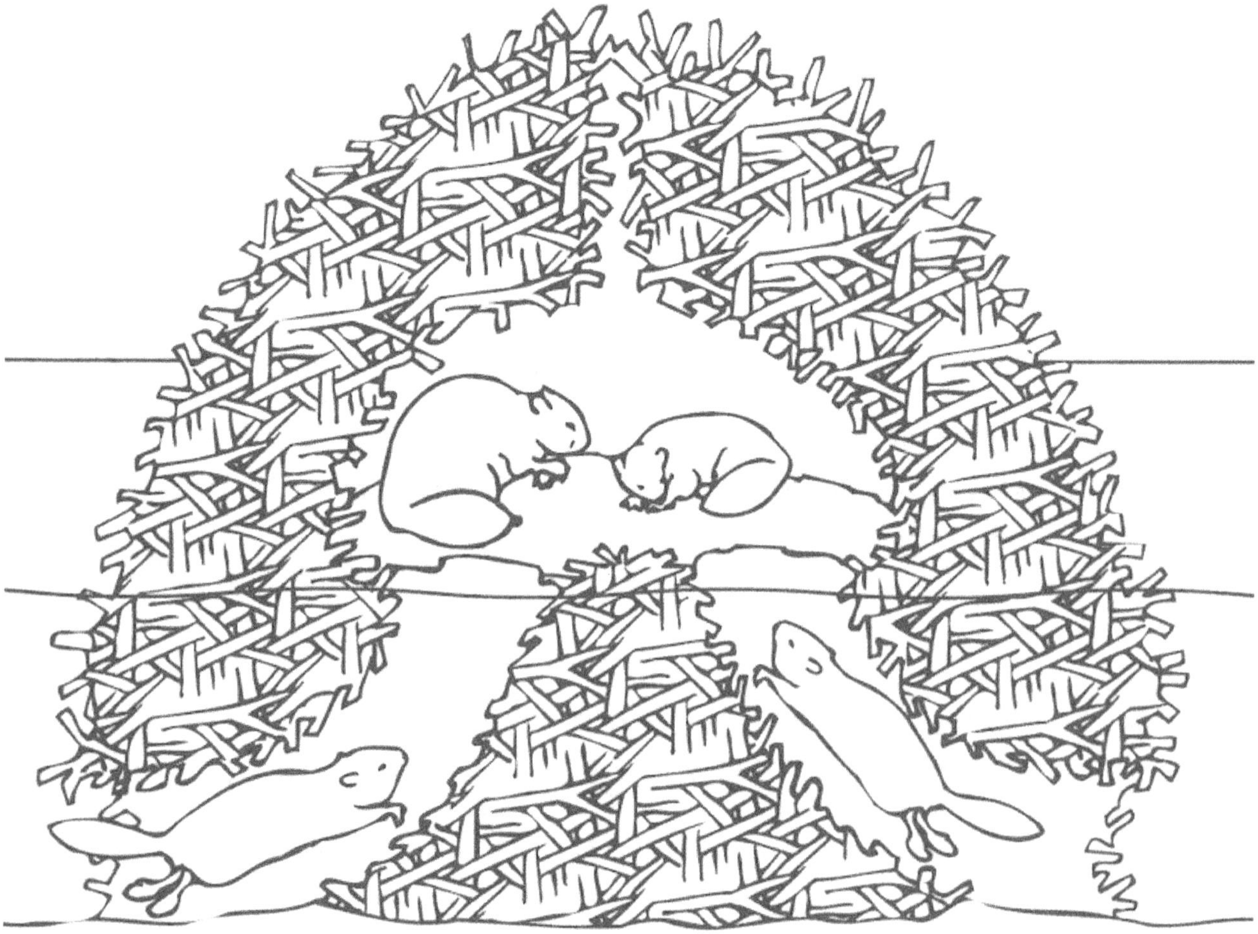

A Legend: "Why Beavers Build Dams"
Told to Hamilton Troll by Boswell & Baxter Beaver

When the first beavers walked the Earth, they lived on land. They gnawed on trees and built their dens, but the wolves would dig them out and the bears could break in.

So a wise She-Beaver sent her children forth to find a safe place to live. They searched the caves but the rocks hurt their feet. They searched the desert but there were no trees and the prickly plants hurt their tender mouths.

One day they happened upon a wide swift running stream; there they decided to rest. However, they were surrounded by their enemies! On one side of the stream there was a pack of wolves, on the other side were bears.

They leapt into the water and swam to the middle of the stream and there they were safe. The wolves and bears saw that they could not get near the beavers so they soon left.

Seeing how they had escaped their enemies the beavers decided that water may be a safe place to live, but how could they raise their cubs and where would they sleep?

Then the youngest beaver had an idea. With the trees they gnawed down and mud gathered and plastered on the trees, they could create their den on water. So they did.

We don't know if the story is true, but our Grand-Pappy told it to us when we were young cubs and now we have told it to you.

Written by: Leigh A. Klug

Definitions & Vocabulary Words:

Gnaw - to chew
Cubs - baby or young beavers
Plaster - to cover a surface with a thick layer of mud

BLUEBIRD

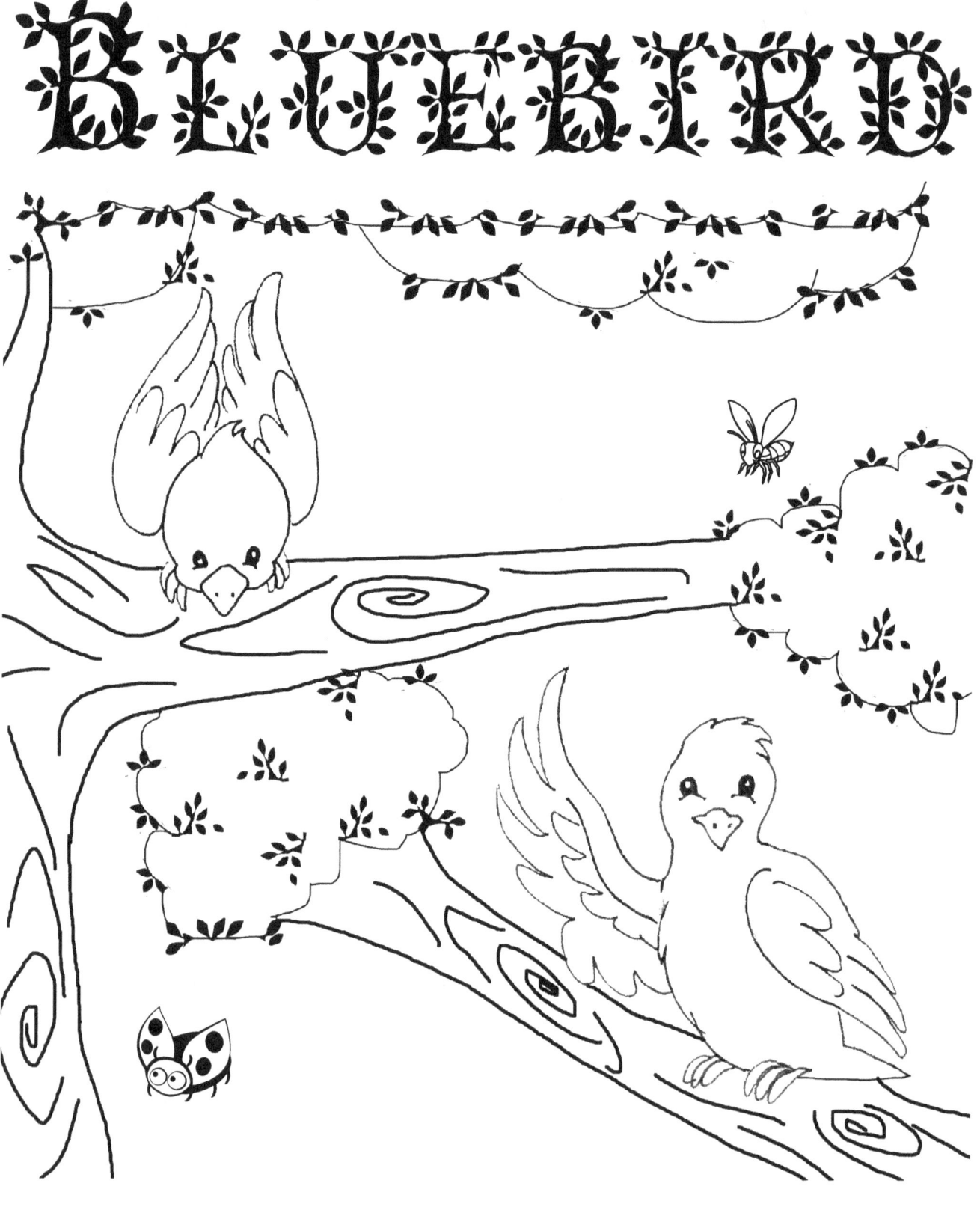

What color are these birds? _____

Do you know the colors of a
RAINBOW?

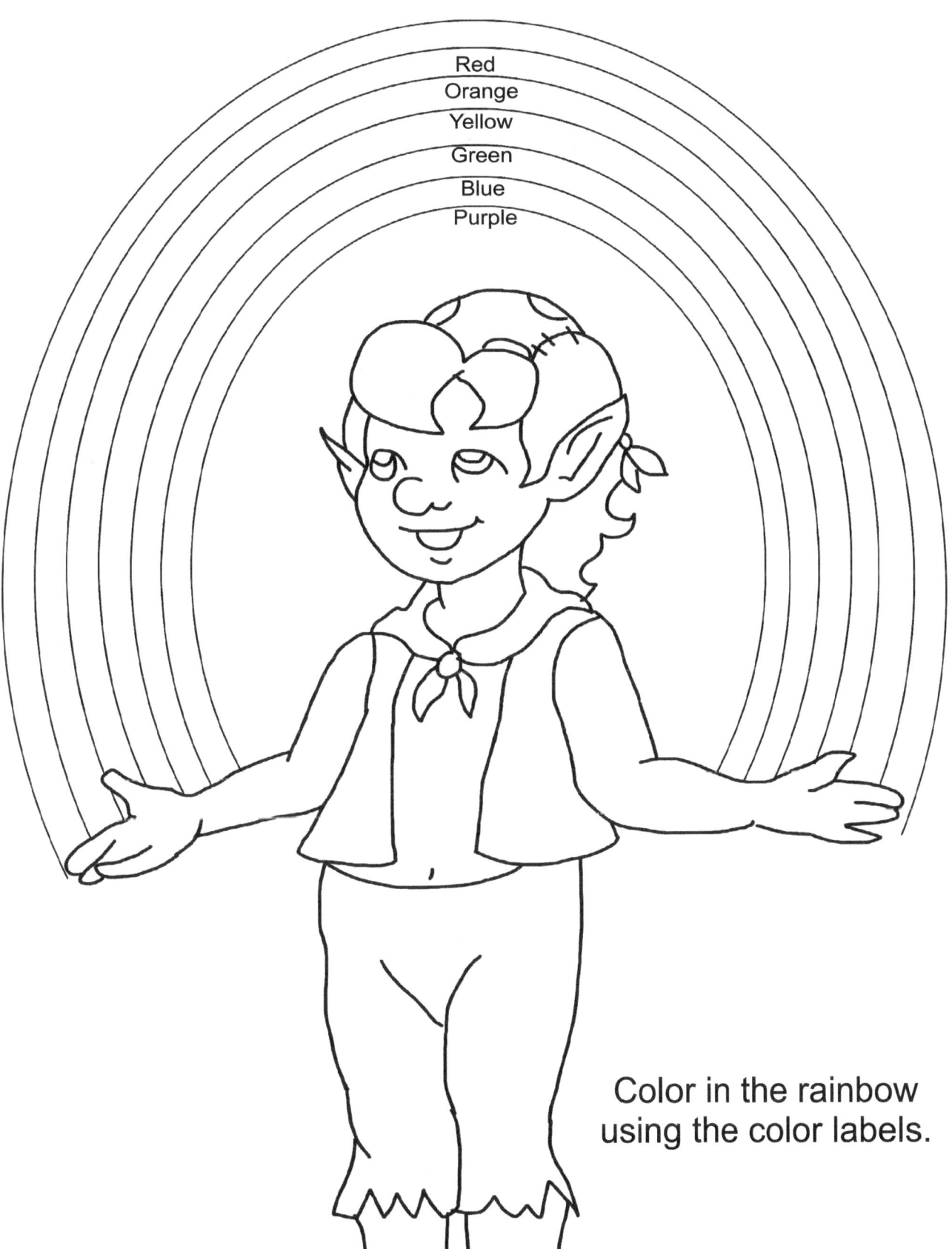

Red
Orange
Yellow
Green
Blue
Purple

Color in the rainbow
using the color labels.

Hamilton Troll loves watching the ants work.

He wishes he could see the tunnels within an ant pile and go inside and explore. But what if he got lost? Help this ant get through the maze by going under and over in the tunnels to get to the other side.

Start

End

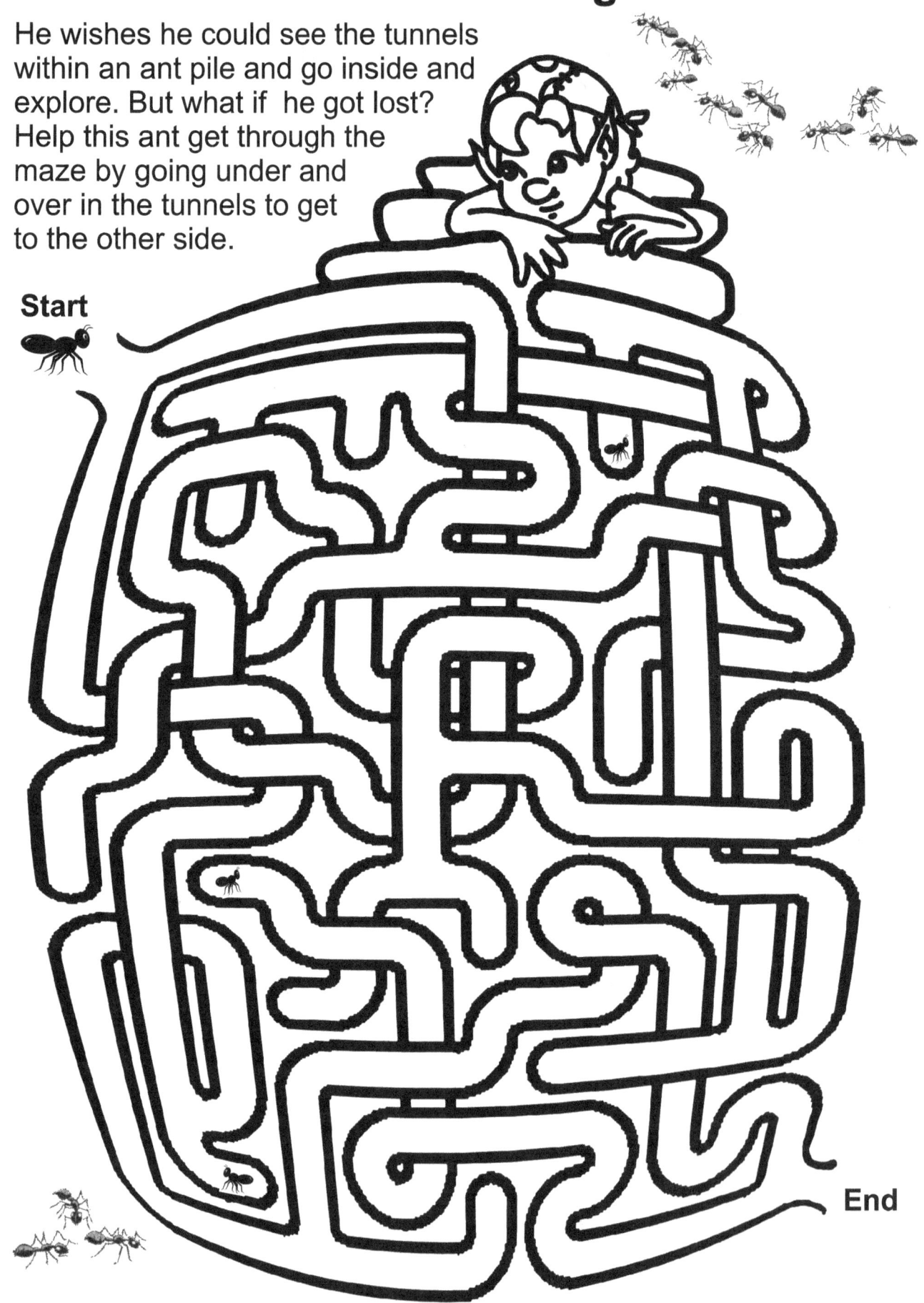

There are now **7** books of the Hamilton Troll series *(and many more to come)*.
In celebration of seven books you must find Hamilton's name in this search **7** times!

HAMILTON

L	I	T	O	N	O	T	L	I	M	A	H
H	A	H	A	M	I	L	T	O	N	O	N
N	A	N	H	A	M	I	N	L	O	T	A
O	M	M	A	H	A	M	I	L	T	O	N
T	I	L	I	H	T	H	A	M	L	T	N
L	L	O	T	L	I	M	A	H	I	T	H
I	I	N	I	N	T	H	A	M	M	N	A
M	M	M	A	H	N	O	T	I	A	O	M
A	A	M	I	L	T	O	N	L	H	T	I
H	H	O	N	O	T	L	I	M	A	H	L

Did you know that trees have rings?

Not like gold rings, but lines that look like circles. These circles are called rings, like you see below, and if you count the rings, you will know how many years that tree had been alive.

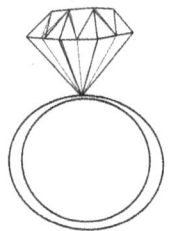

Make your way through this tree stumps rings to get to the center.

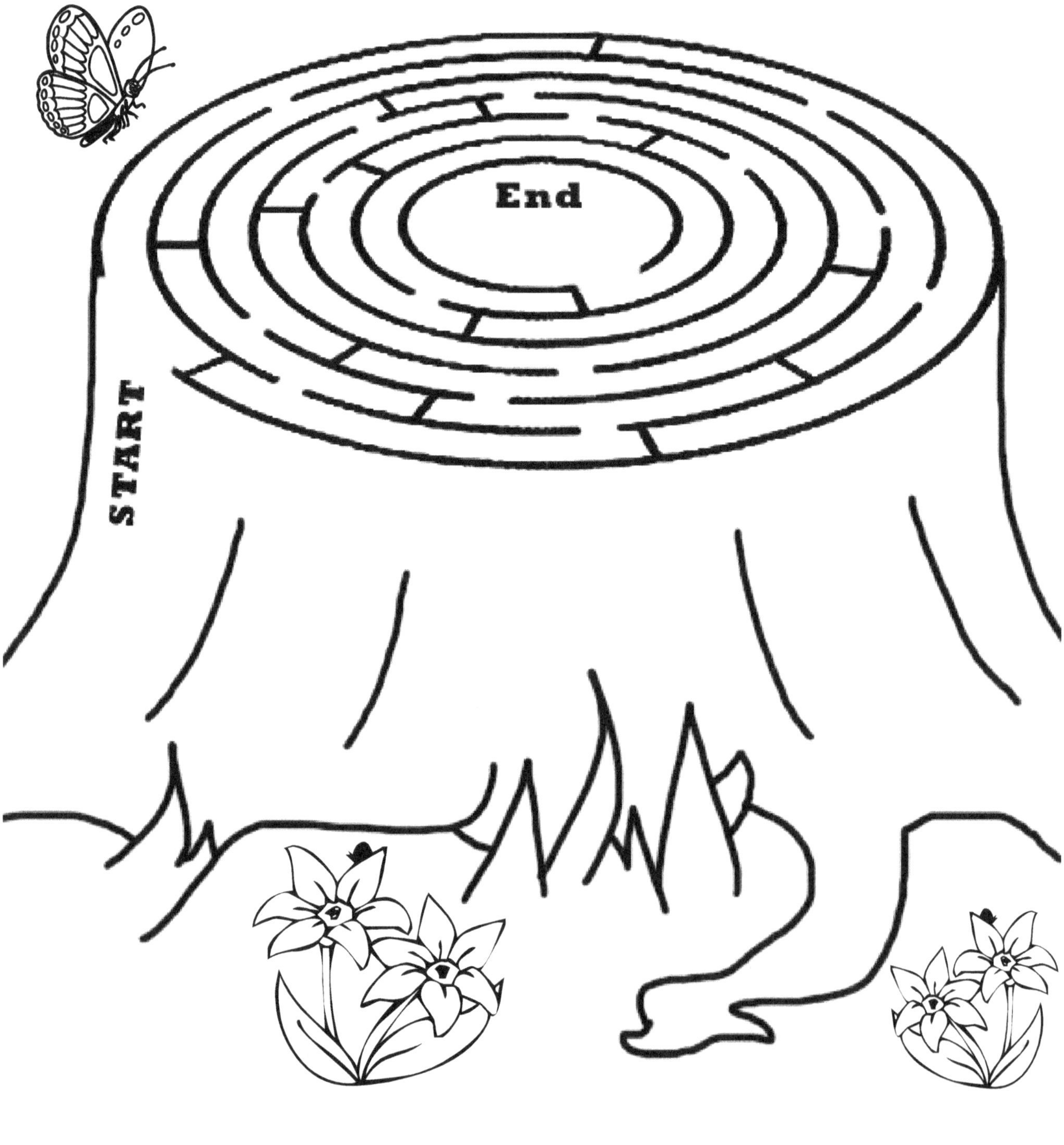

START

End

Hamilton Troll wants to know, what YOU are thinking about.

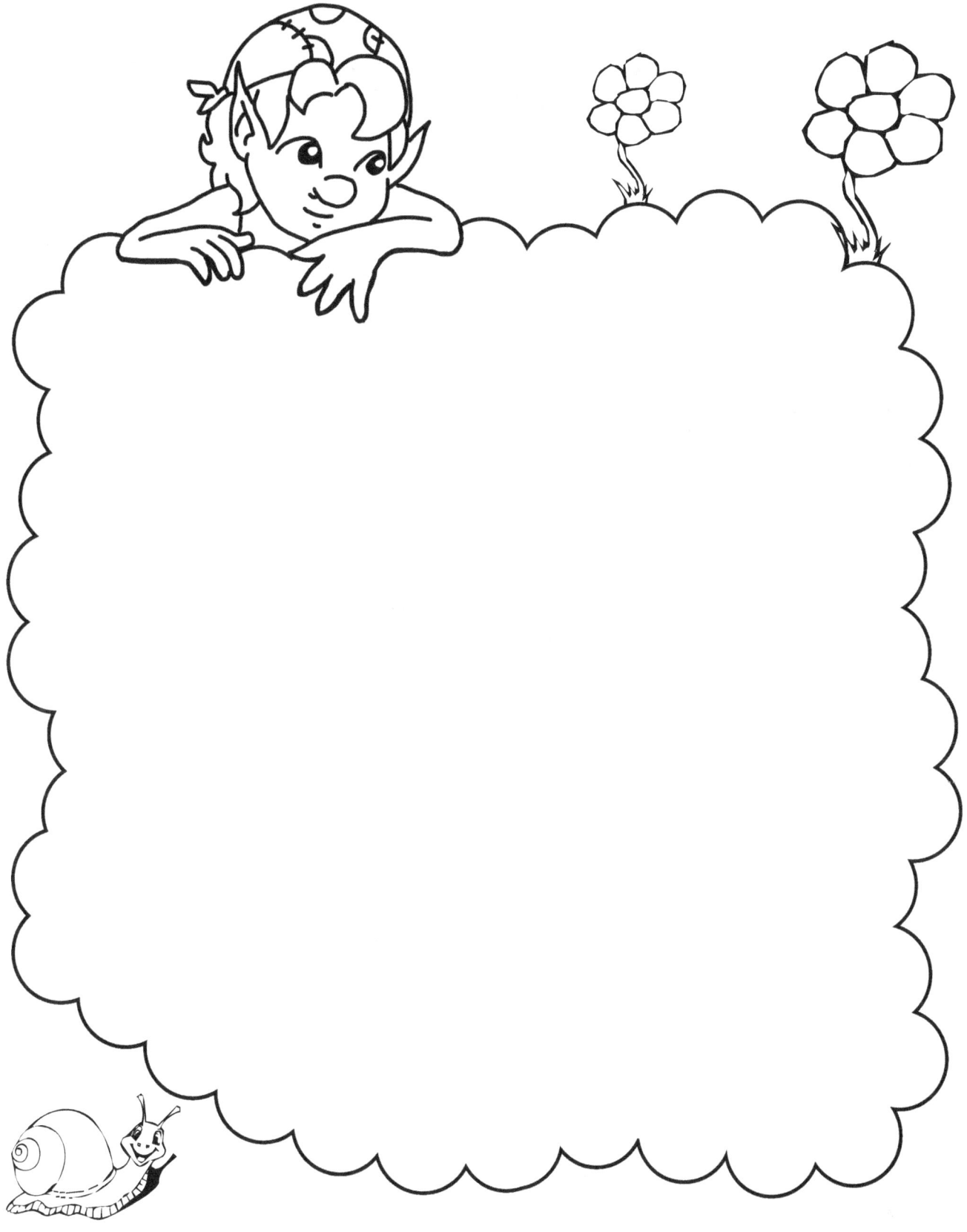

Why do FROGS make the BEST Cheerleaders?

1. They jump real high.

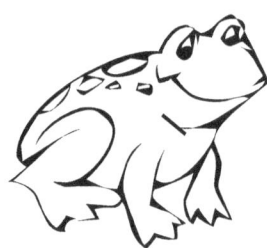 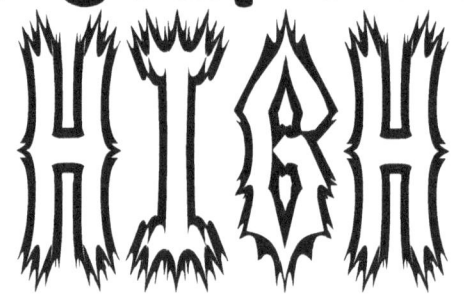 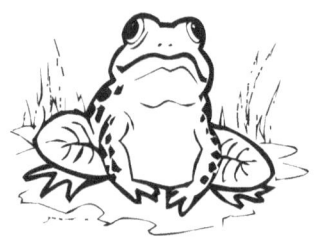

2. They croak real loud.

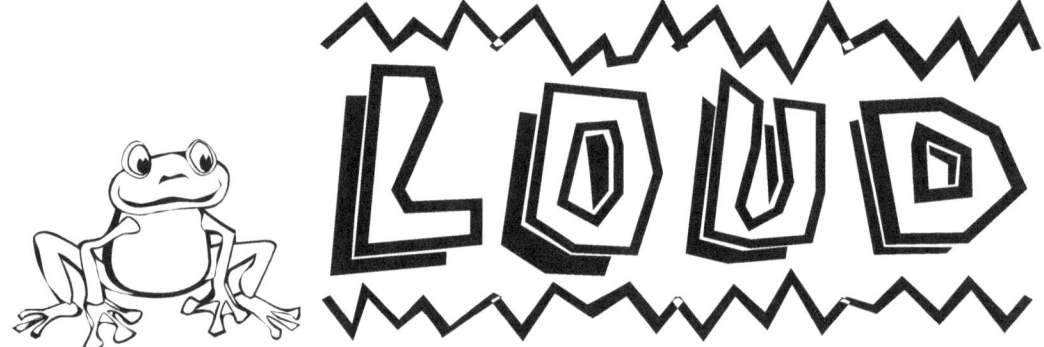

3. They move real fast.

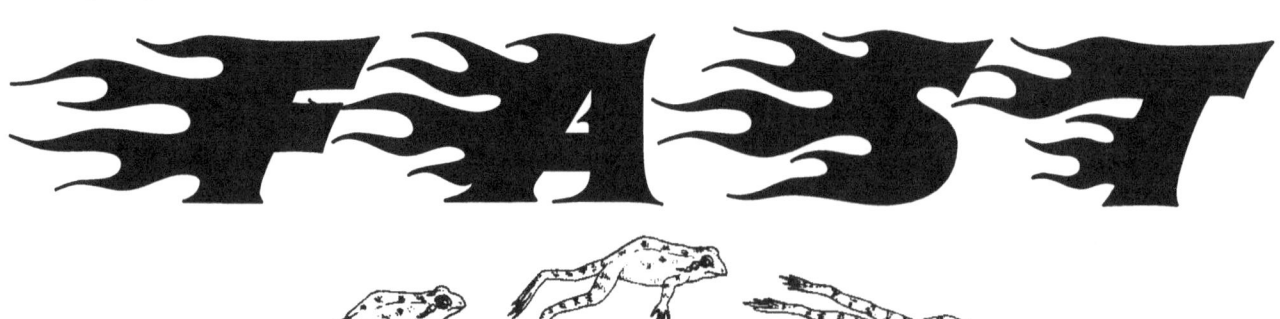

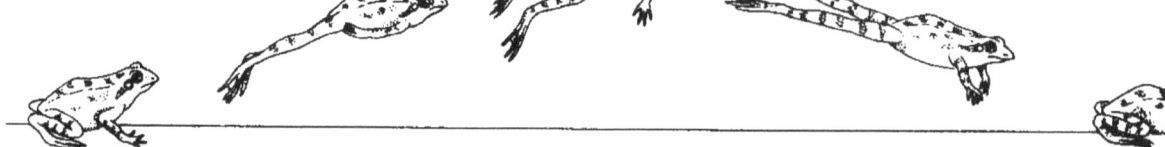

Hip-Hip-Hooray!

Give me a
T...

Give me
an R...

Give me
an O...

Give me
an L...

Give me
an L...

What does that spell?
TROLL!

DID YOU KNOW?
FROGS

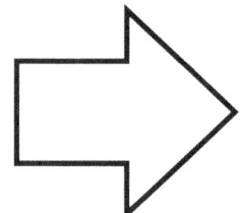 **Frogs don't drink; they absorb water through their skin.**

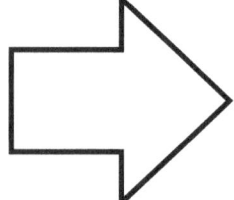 **The smallest known frog is about ½ inch long, and the largest known frog is about a foot long.**

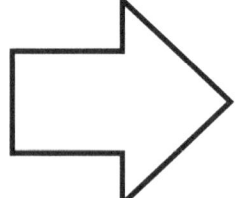 **There are over 4,000 frog species in the world, with only 88 of them in the United States.**

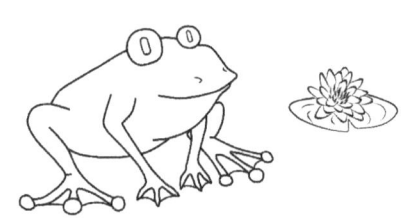
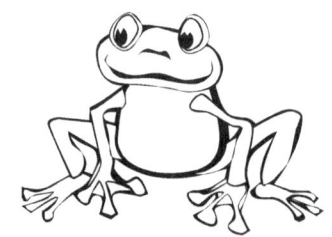
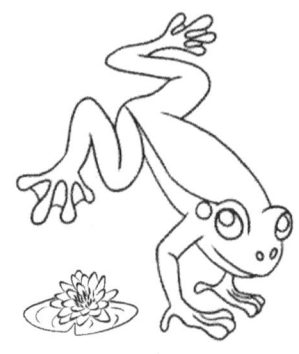

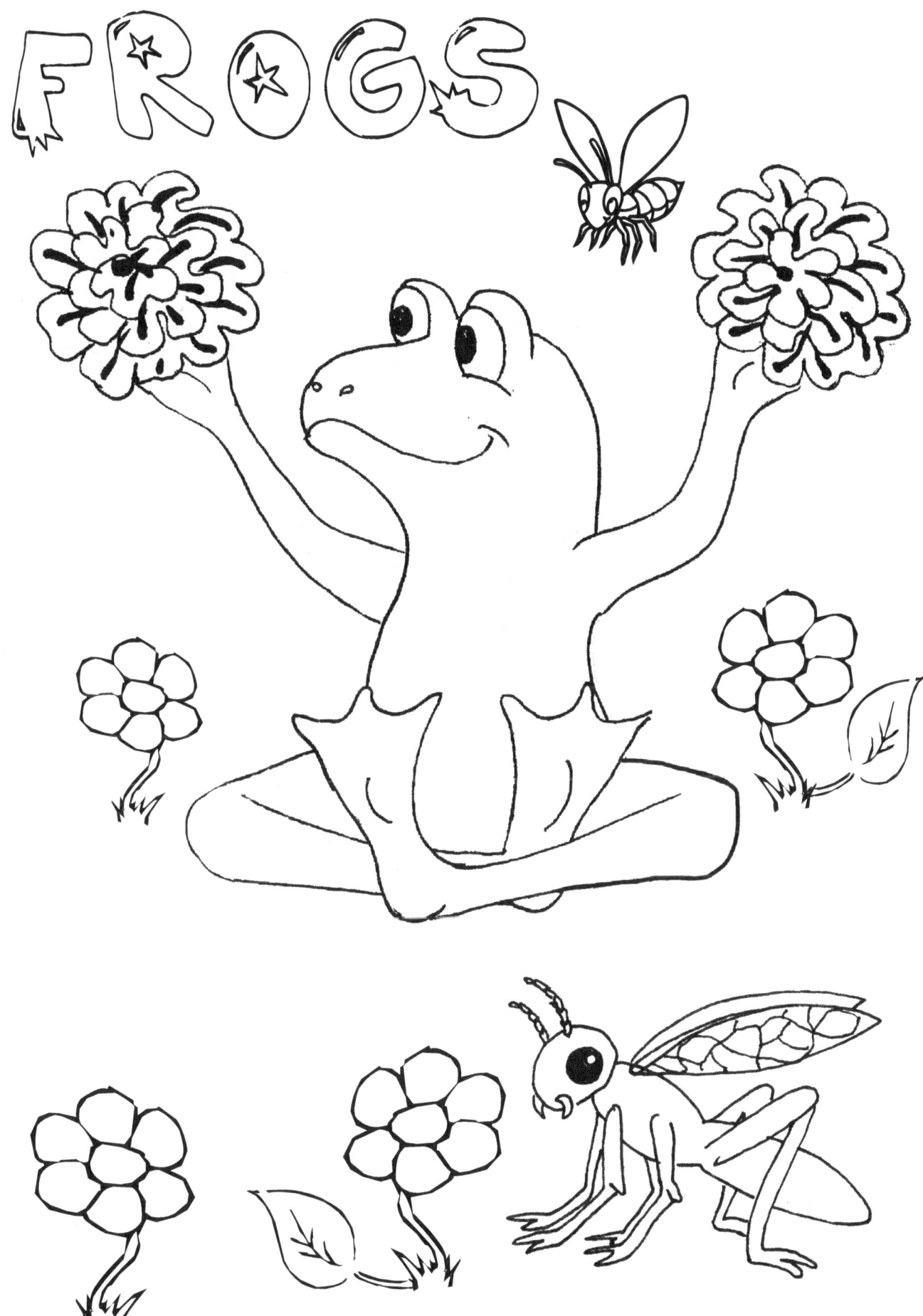

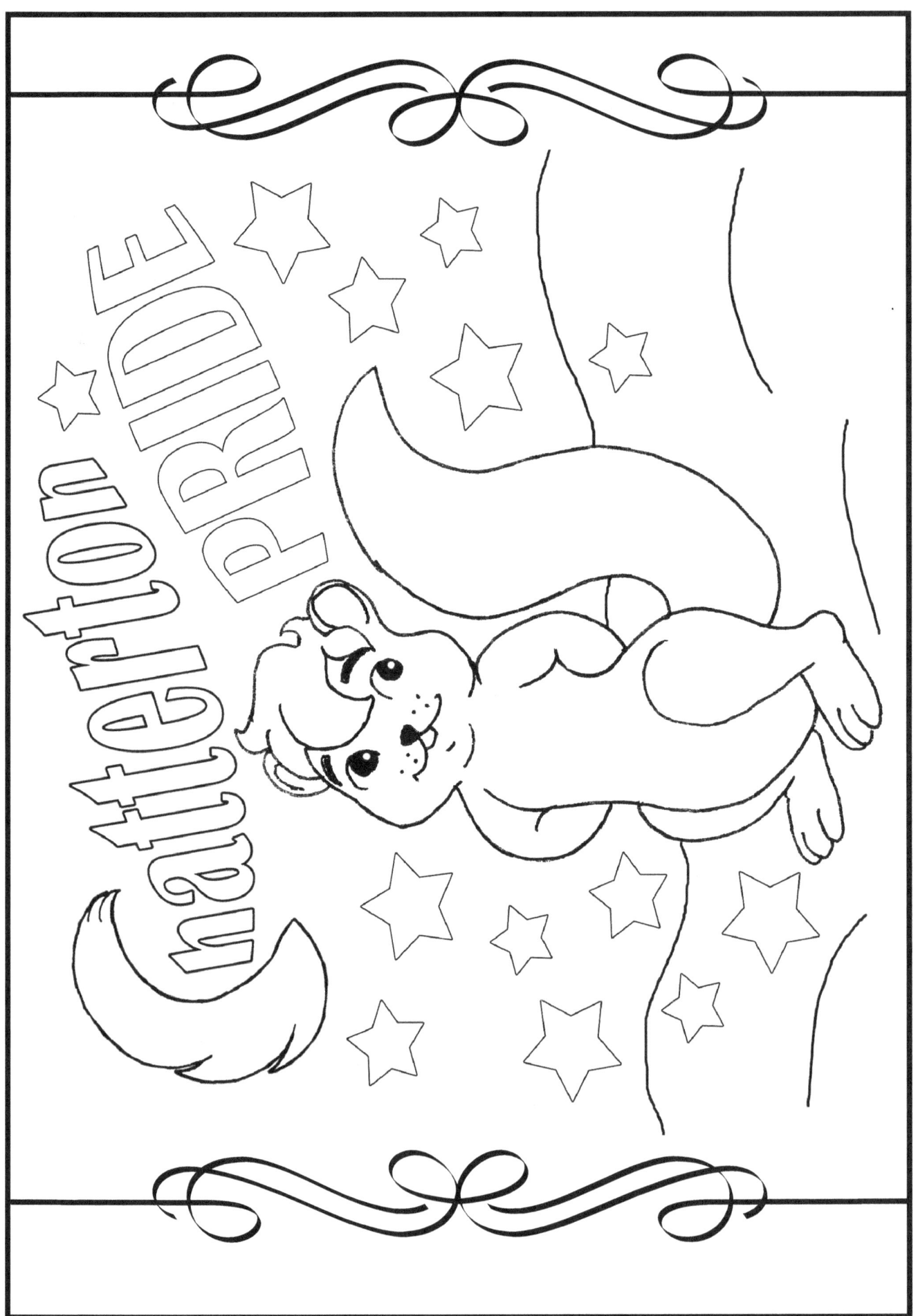

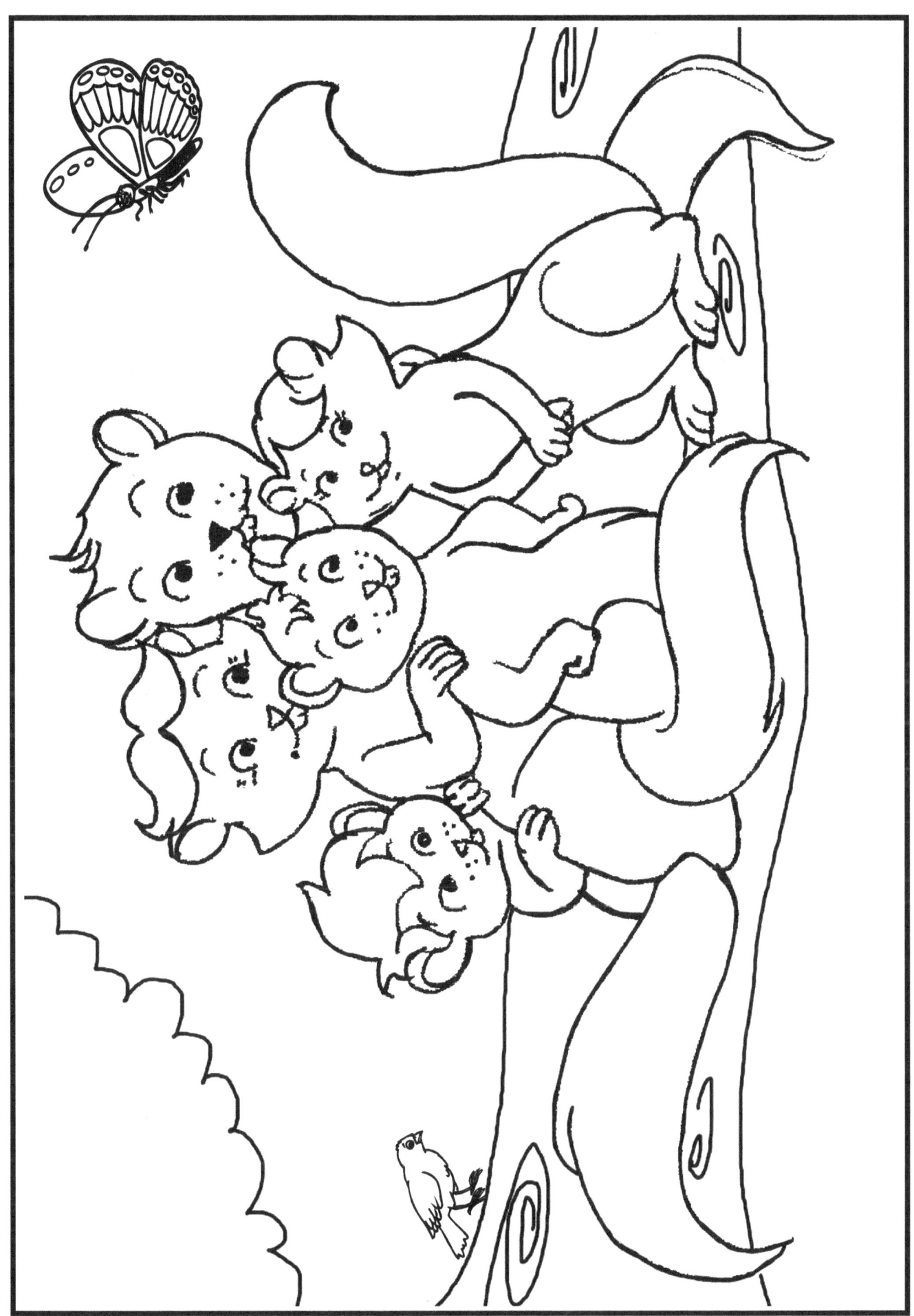

N	A	N	O	T	R	E	C	H	A	T	N
C	A	T	O	O	N	C	H	A	R	O	O
T	H	R	E	N	C	A	R	T	T	N	T
R	H	E	T	R	T	O	O	R	O	C	R
E	R	T	R	E	H	O	E	A	N	H	E
T	H	T	E	T	R	T	N	H	T	A	T
A	T	T	A	T	T	T	H	C	E	T	A
H	A	A	R	A	T	R	O	N	R	T	A
C	R	H	H	C	H	A	T	T	R	O	H
T	A	C	H	A	T	E	R	T	O	N	C

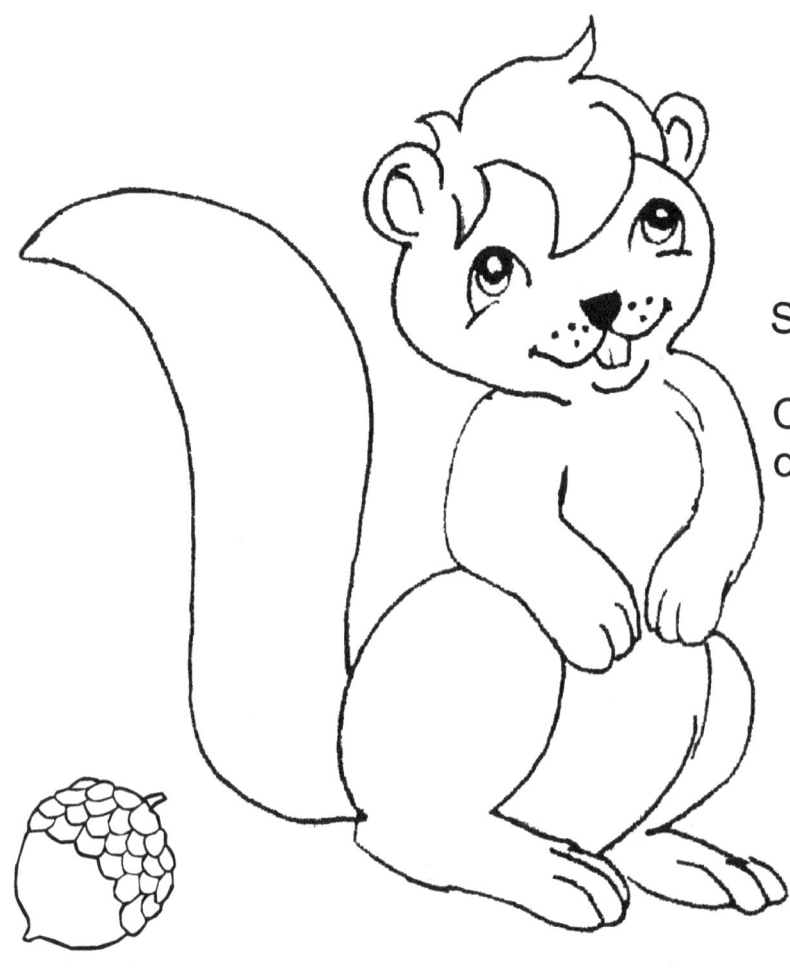

There is only one Chatterton Squirrel just like there is only one of you!

So this word search puzzle is a little different. The name Chatterton can only be found one time in the entire puzzle!

Can you find it?

CHATTERTON

1

Draw a Picture for Chatterton Squirrel!

Chatterton can't wait to see what you will draw for him. Draw anything you want in the box. Then share it with someone special.

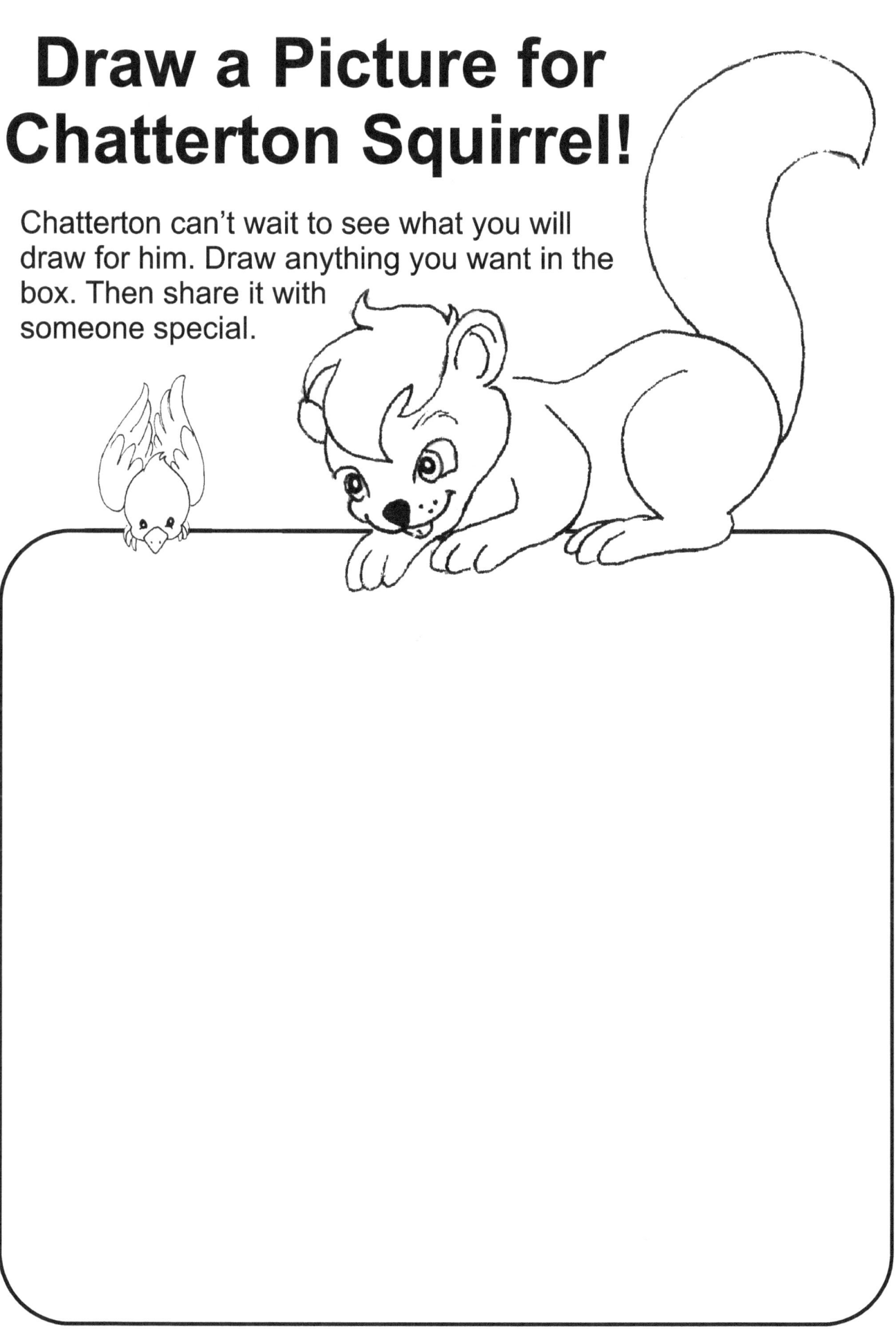

Rachet Raccoon

DID YOU KNOW?
RACCOONS

➡ Raccoons climb trees when they feel threatened. They also make their homes in old tree hollows (holes).

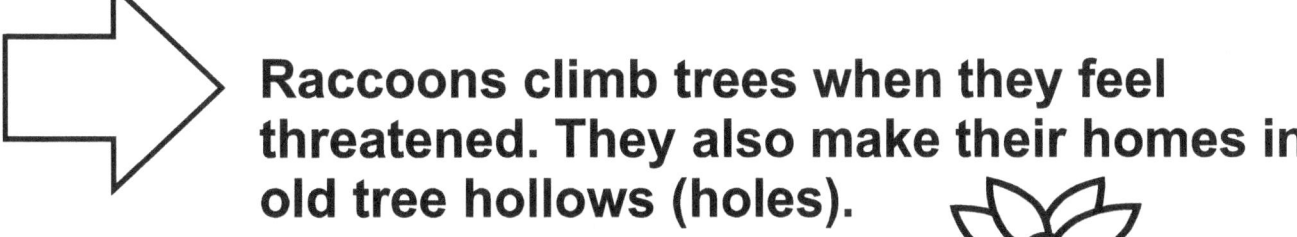

➡ Raccoons have been known to clean their food.

➡ They are very smart at solving problems and have been known to remember solutions for up to three years.

➡ They do not wear masks but their eyes are surrounded by brown/black fur.

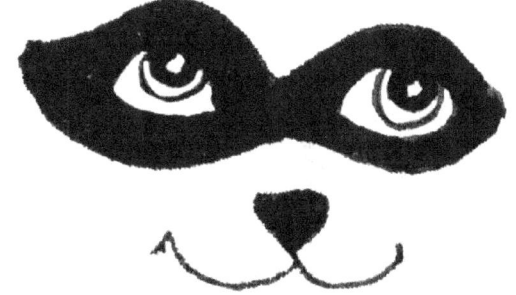

BUTTERFLIES

DID YOU KNOW?

Butterflies

➡️ Butterflies have lived on Earth about 50 million years.

➡️ They have four large brightly colored wings that are made of soft scales.

➡️ Butterflies start out as caterpillars that eat leaves until they go into their cocoon and emerge later as a butterfly.

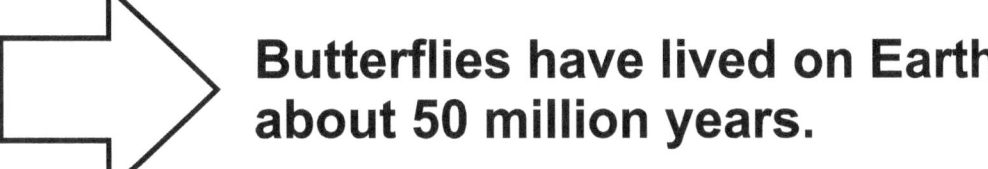

➡️ Butterflies eat nectar and pollen from flowers, along with tree sap and rotting fruit.

➡️ Butterflies migrate (travel) as much as 3000 miles per year.

➡️ There are about 20,000 species (types) of butterflies in the world!

DID YOU KNOW?

Mushroom

→ Mushrooms are also called toadstools.

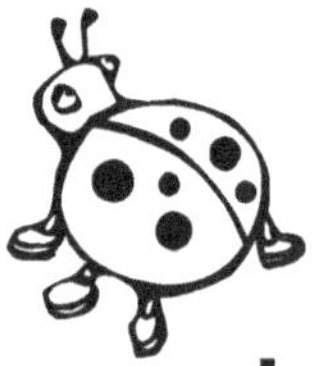

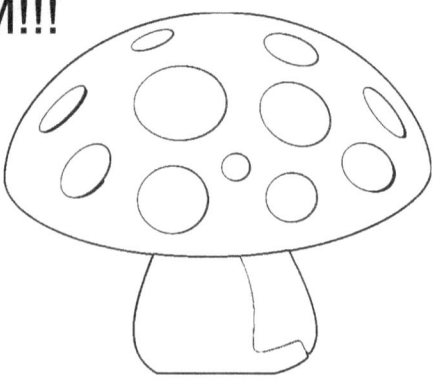

→ Some mushrooms seem to appear overnight, although it takes them a couple days to appear.

→ A mushroom is a fungi (type of fungus) not to be confused with being a 'fun guy'.

→ There are over 5000 types of mushrooms of different shapes, colors and sizes. Some can be eaten, some can not.

NEVER
EAT A WILD
MUSHROOM!!!

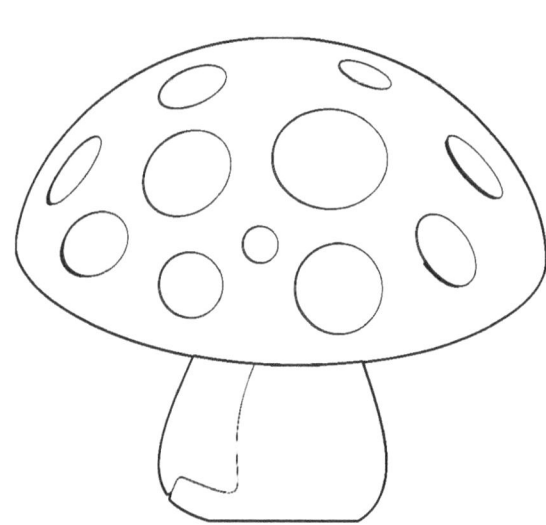
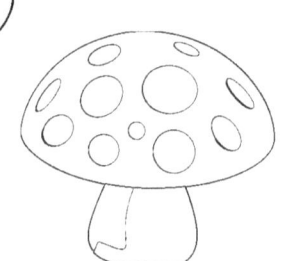

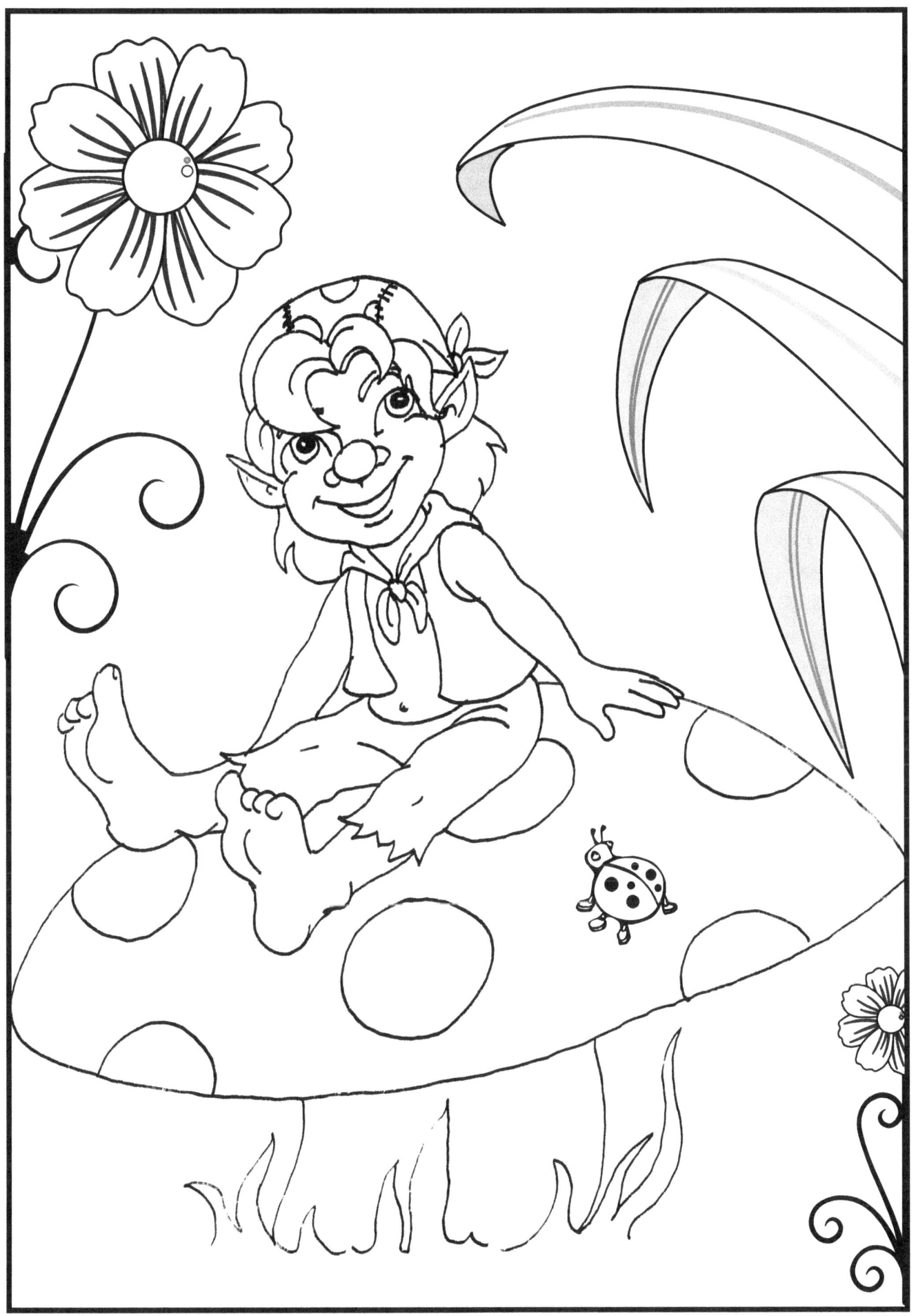

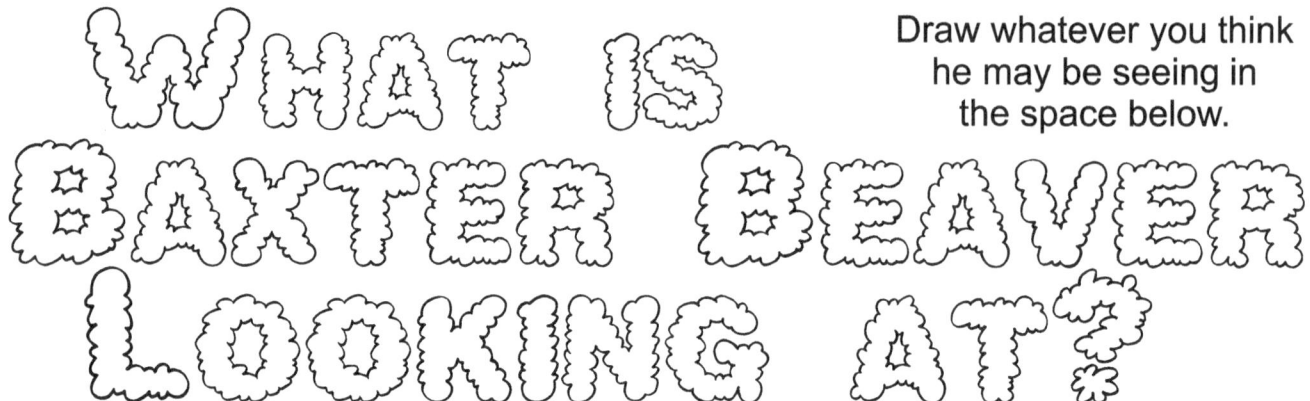

WHAT IS BAXTER BEAVER LOOKING AT?

Draw whatever you think he may be seeing in the space below.

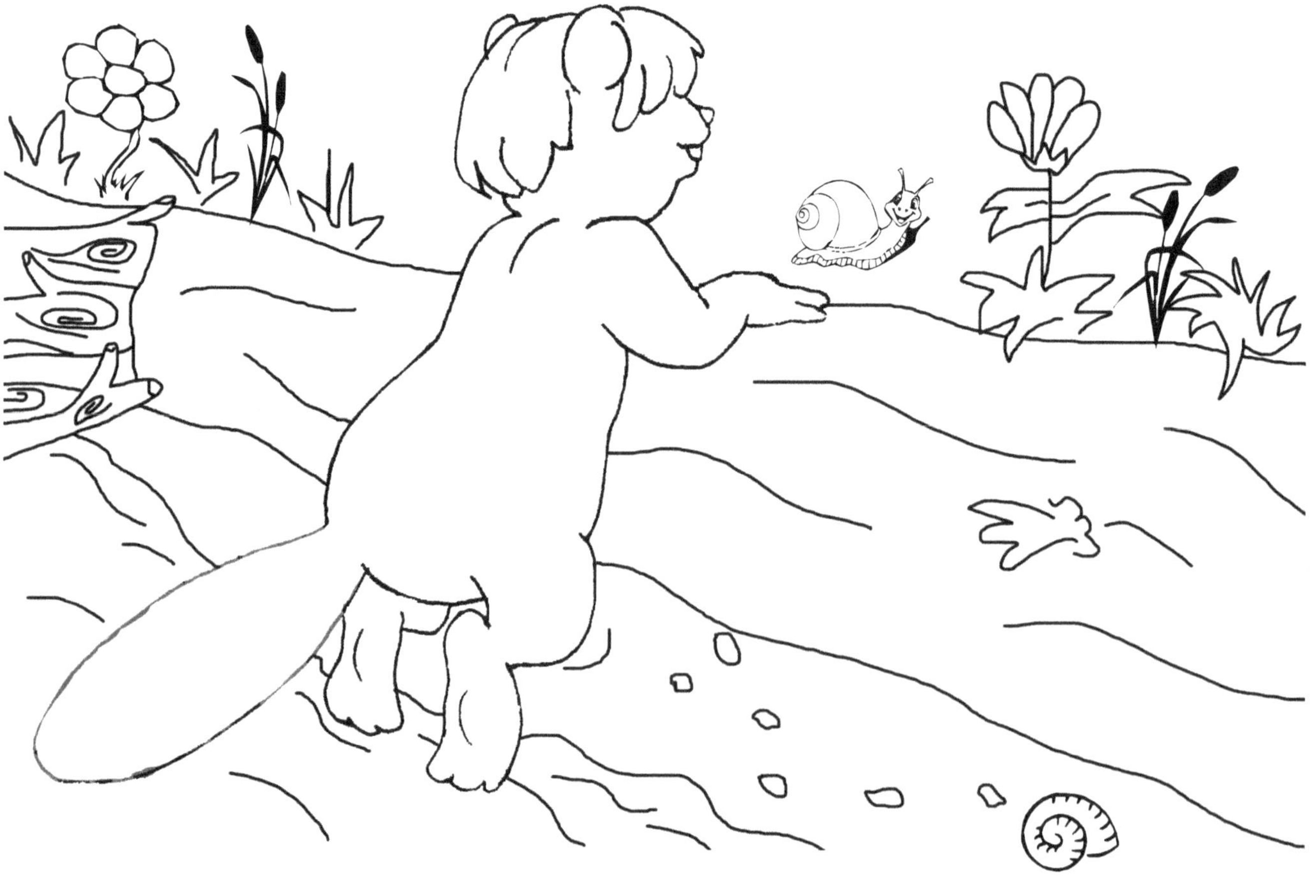

BEAVERS SWIM IN WATER

What else swims in water?
Draw it below.

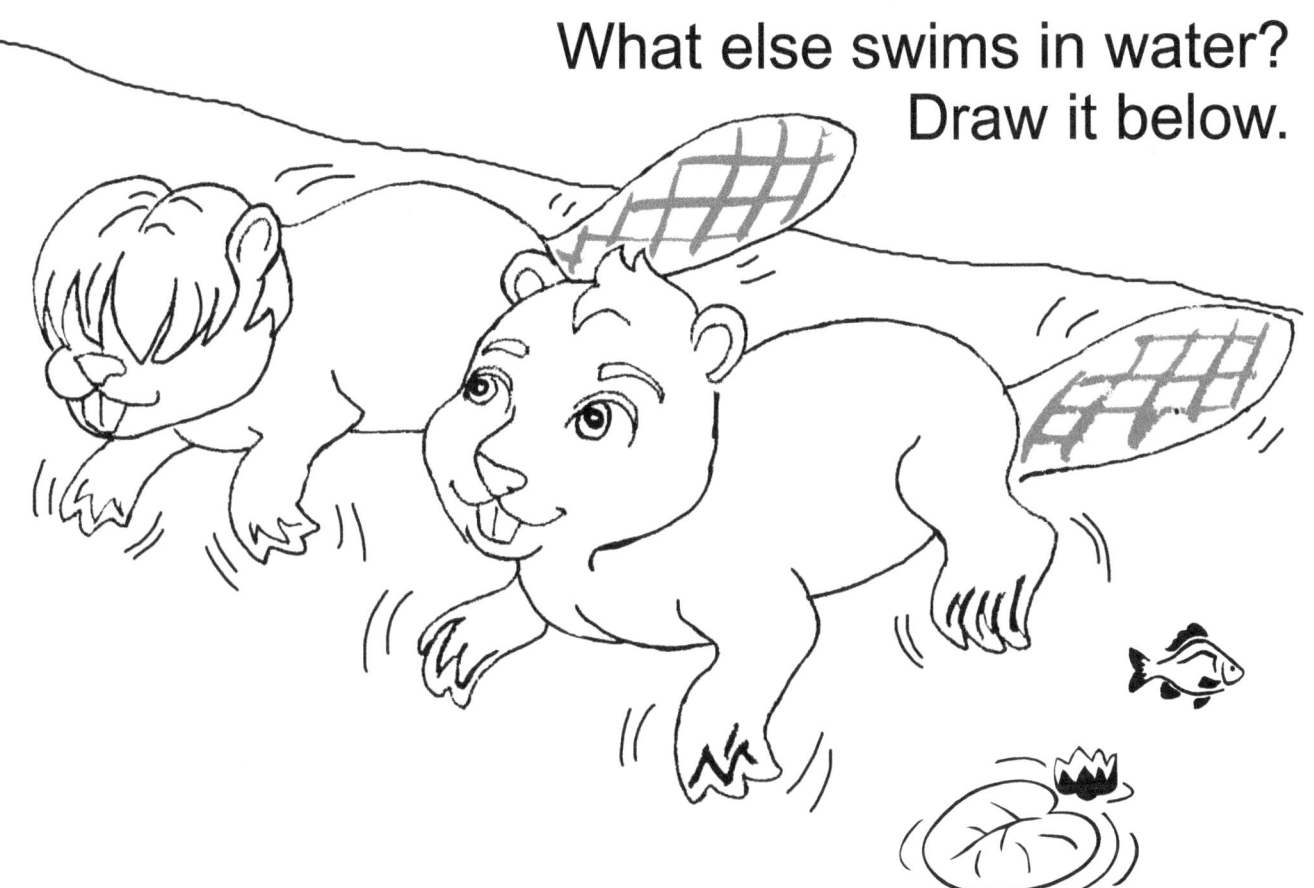

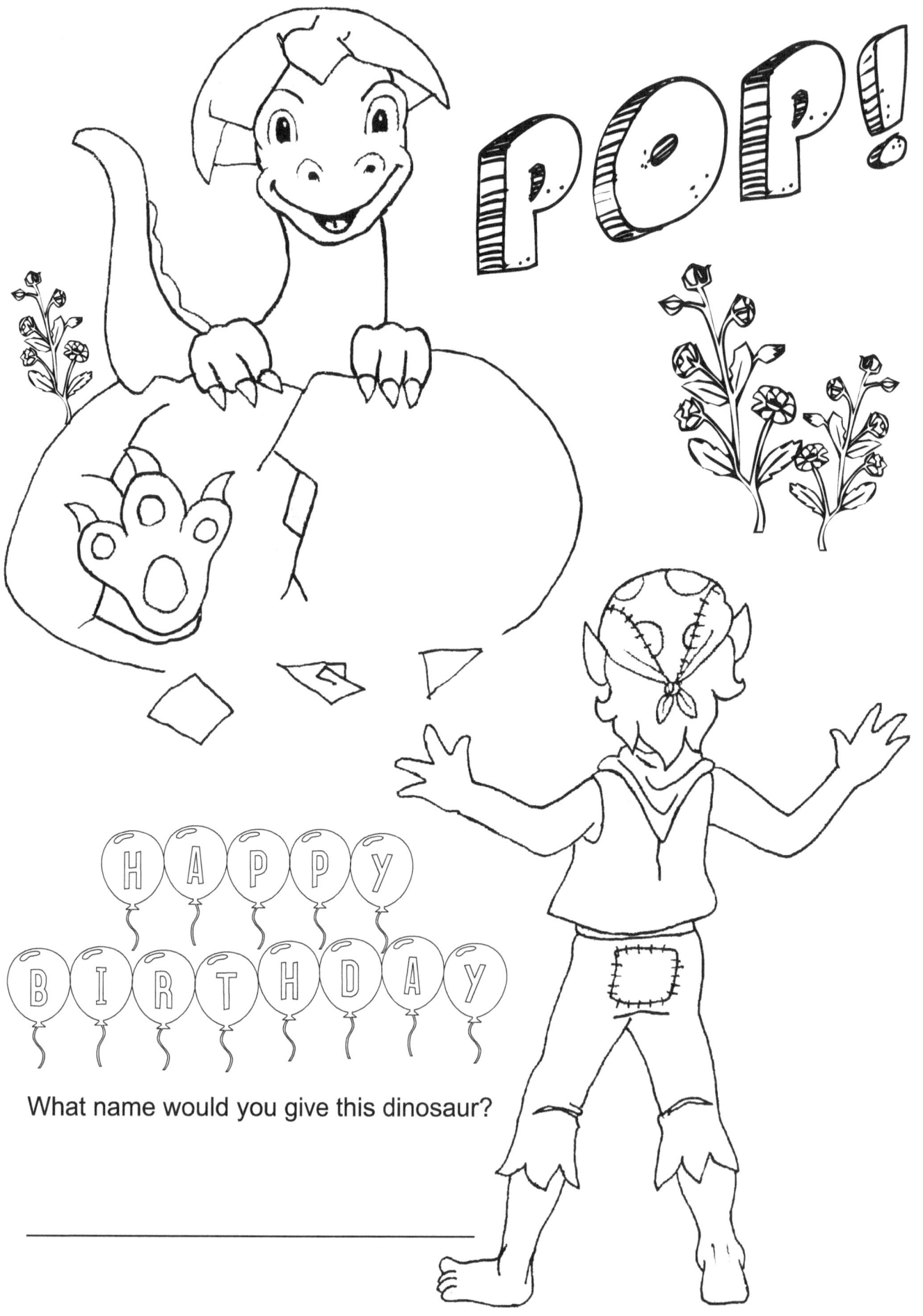

What name would you give this dinosaur?

_____

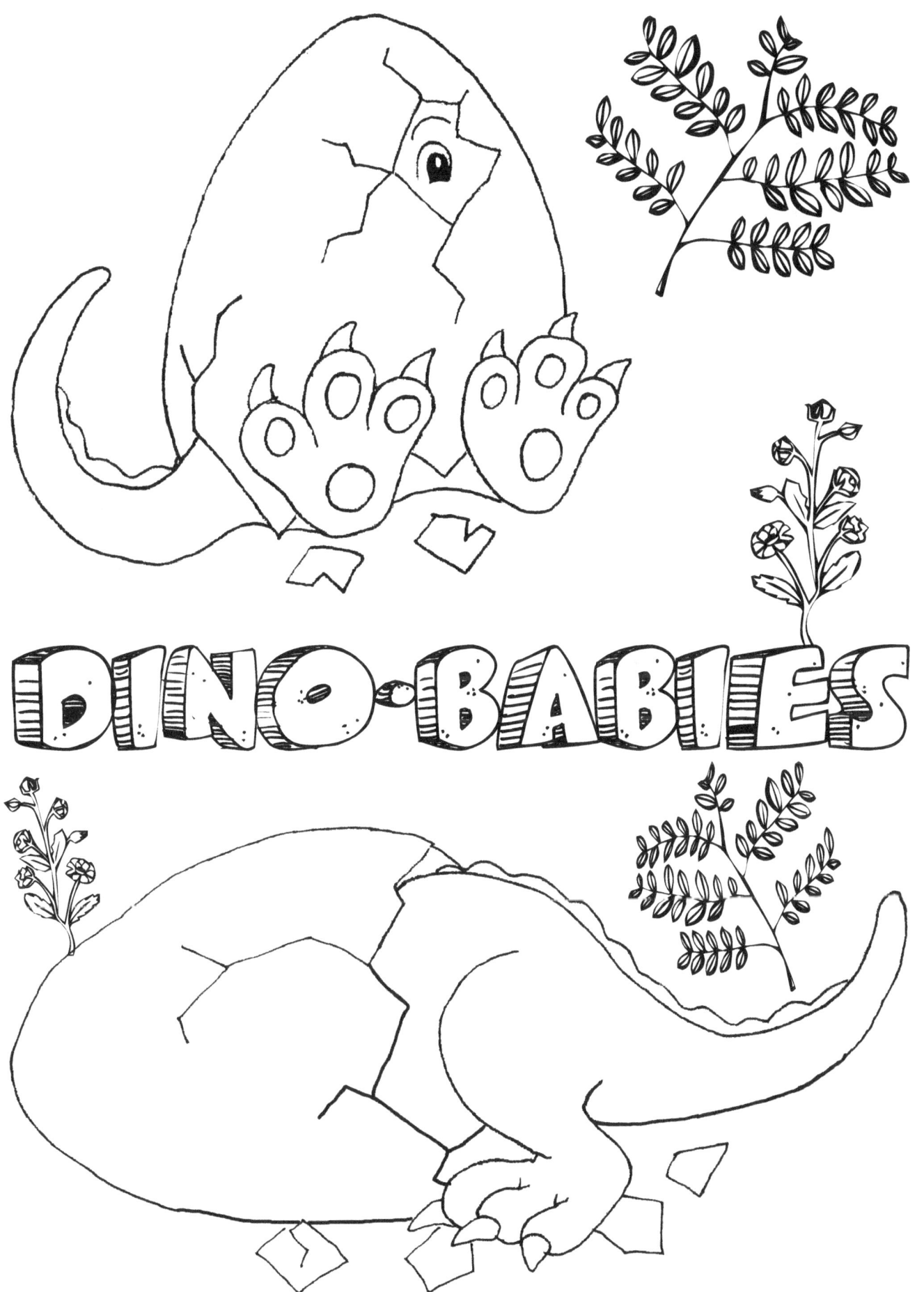

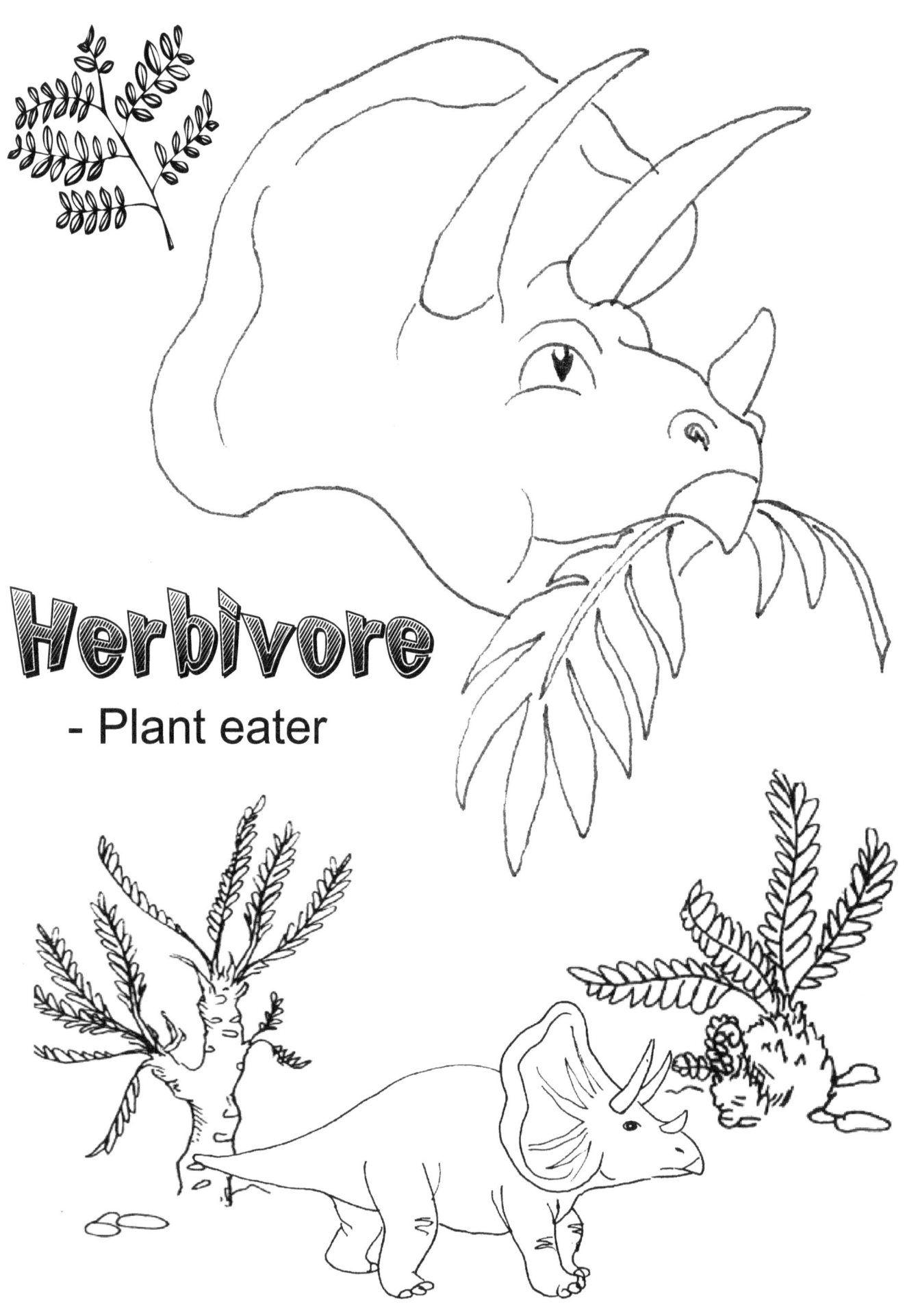

Herbivore

- Plant eater

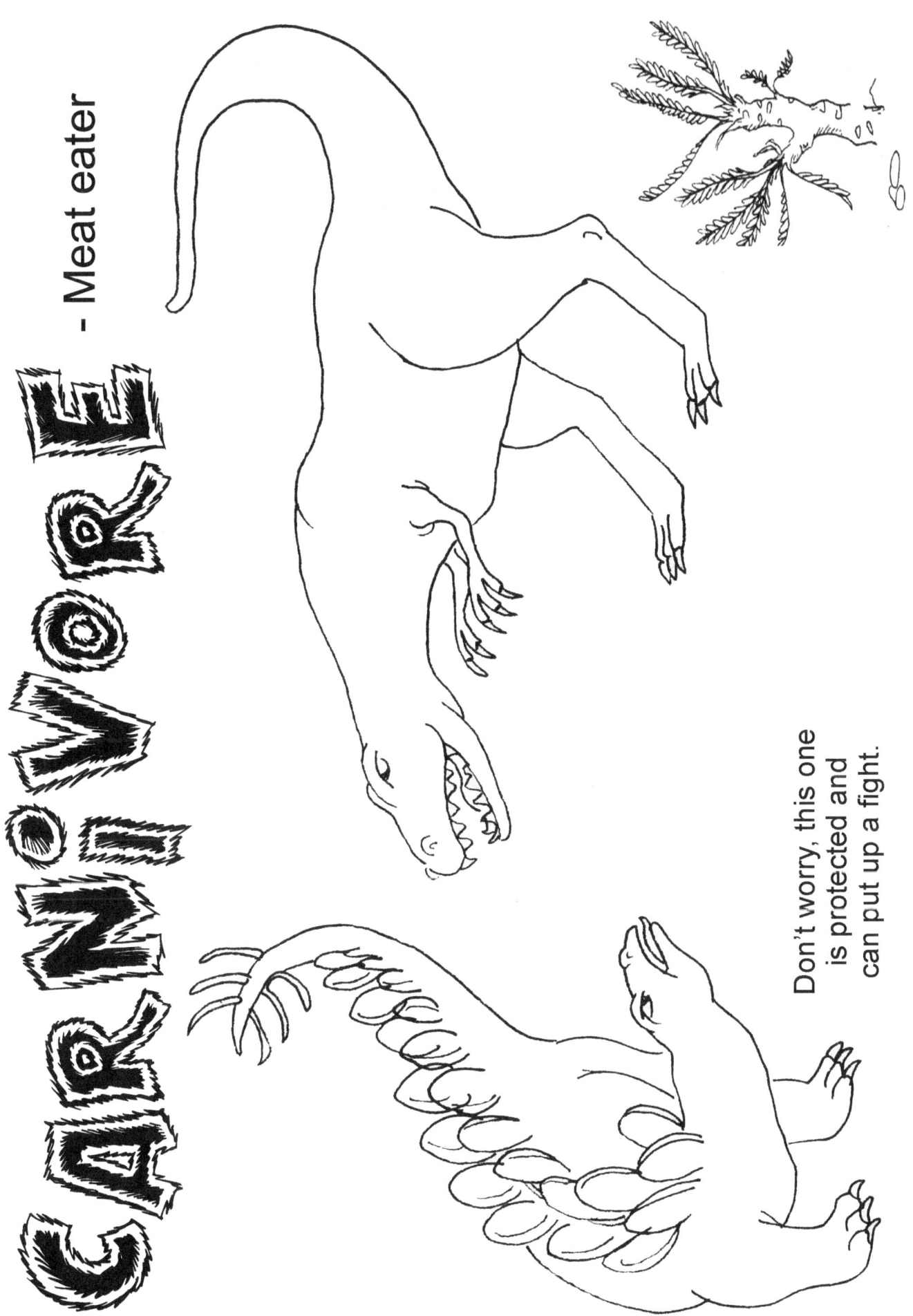

CARNIVORE

- Meat eater

Don't worry, this one
is protected and
can put up a fight.

DINOSAURS

There are so many, let's just name a few.

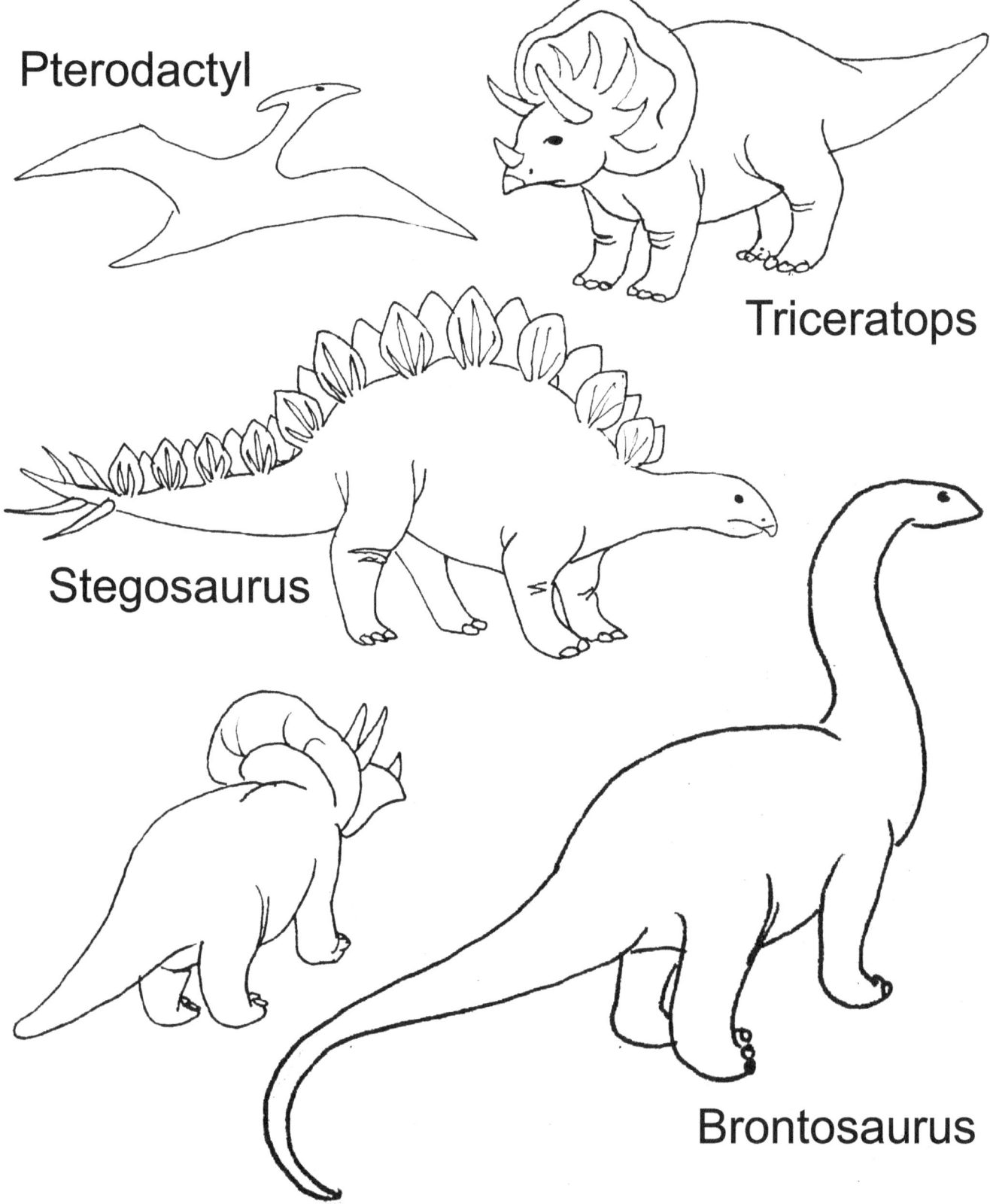

Pterodactyl

Triceratops

Stegosaurus

Brontosaurus

Which one is Which?

Draw a line from the words to the correct dinosaur.

Herbivore   Carnivore

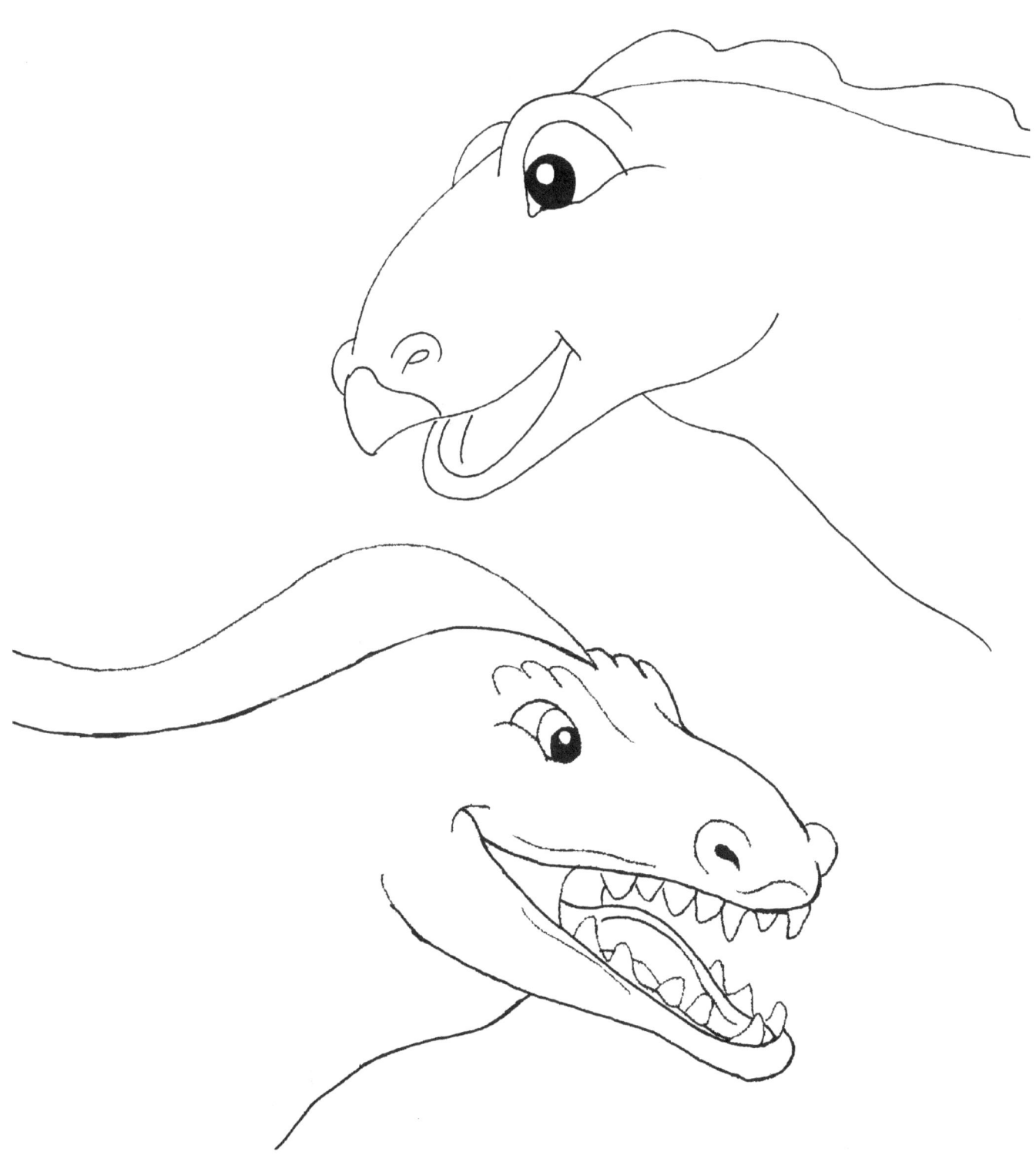

Raccoons are NOCTURNAL
meaning they only come out at night.

What do you think Rachel Racoon is looking at tonight?
What do YOU usually see at night?

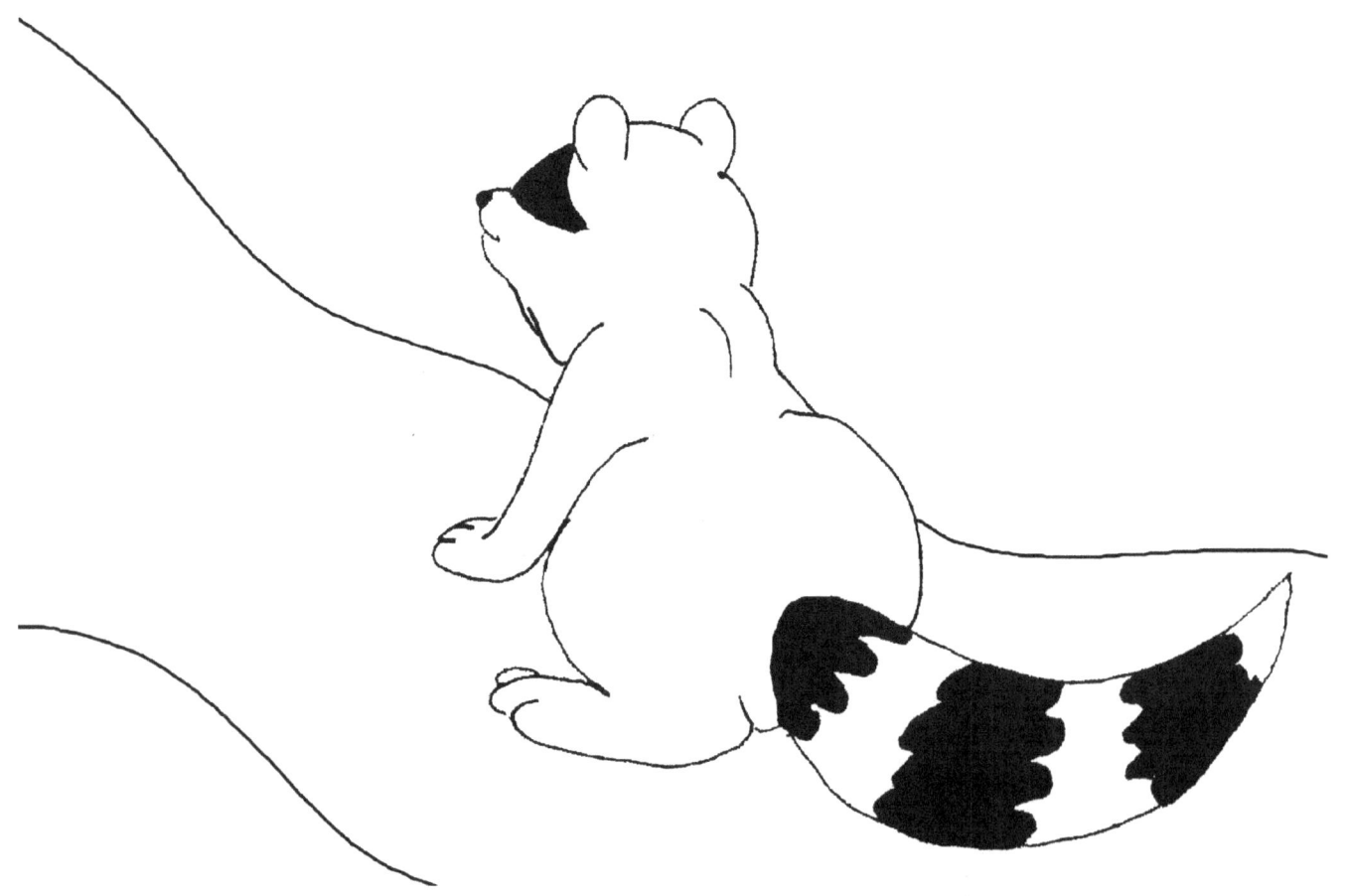

What is the MOUSE thinking about?

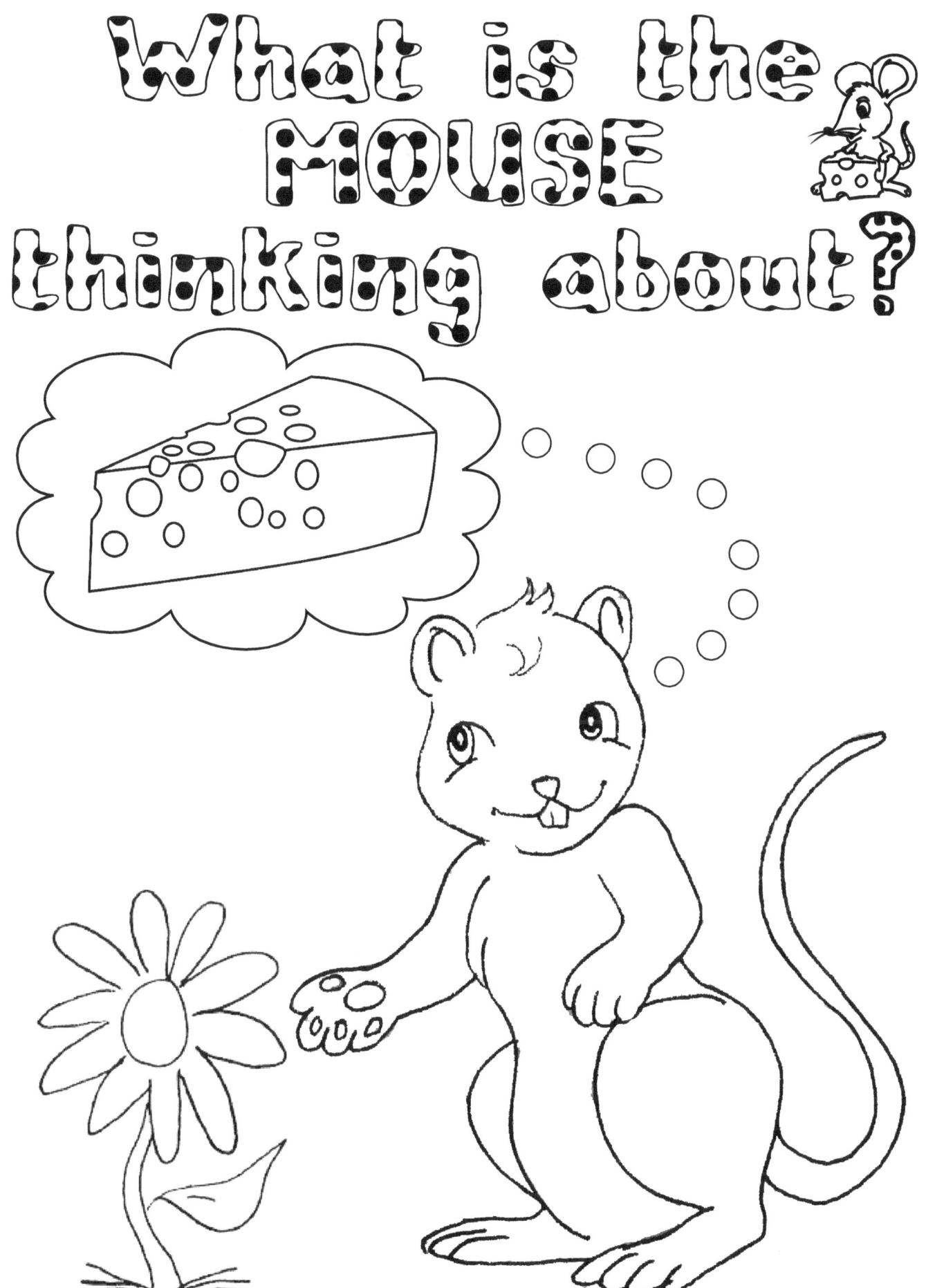

WHAT IS HAMILTON TROLL AND WHITAKER OWL LOOKING AT?

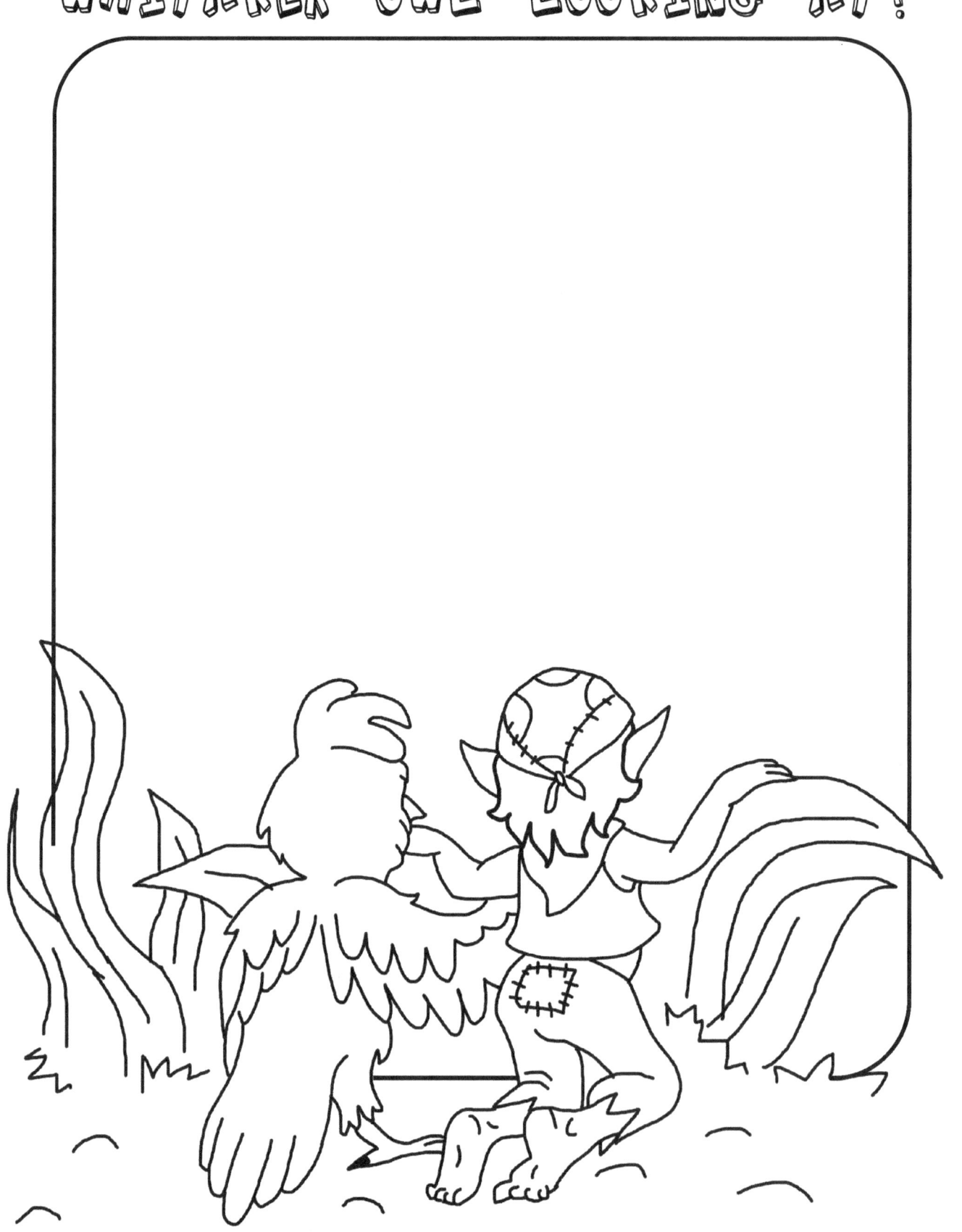

DIFFERENT

One of these Chatterton Squirrel's are different.
Can you circle which one?

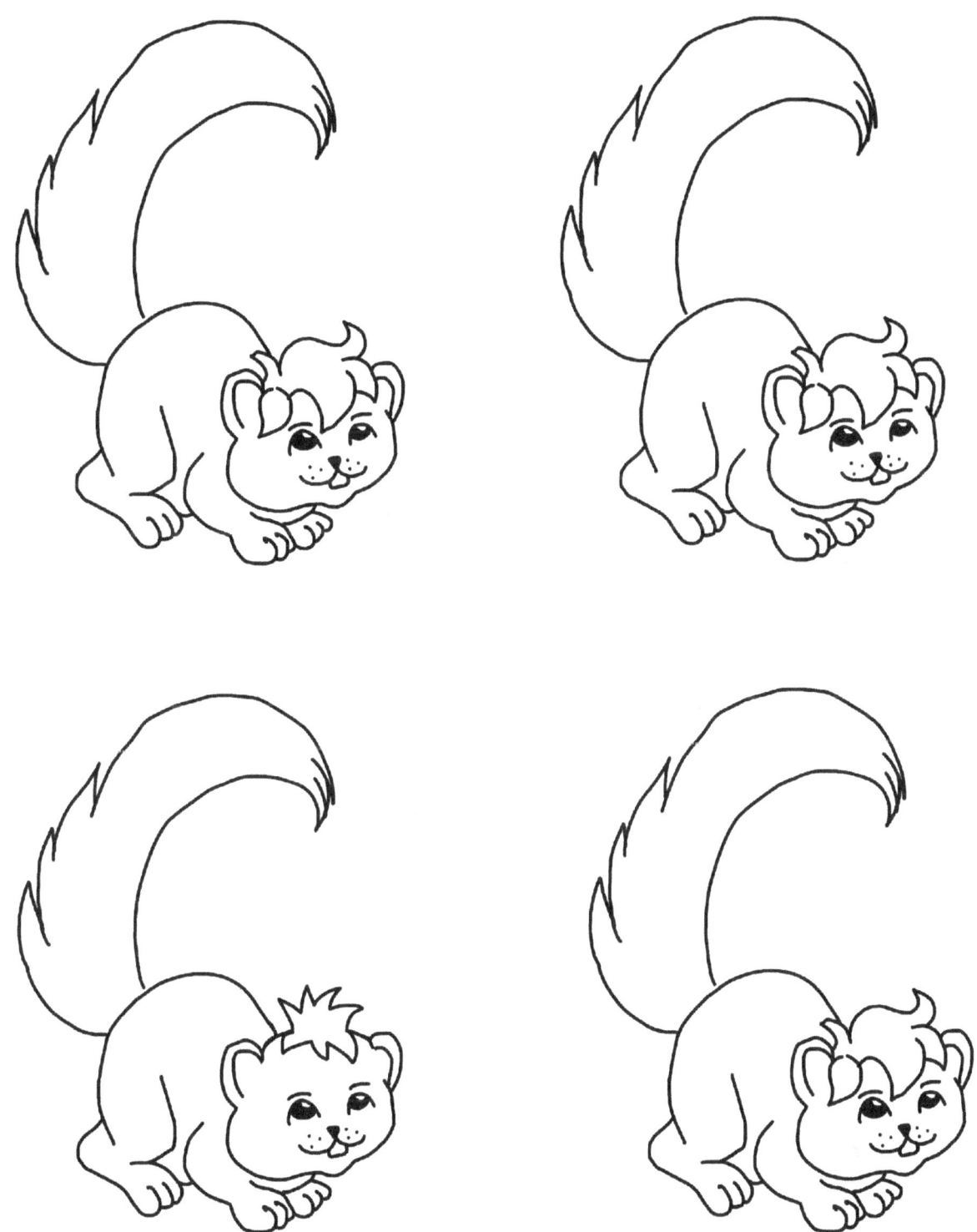

STICK NUT PITCHER

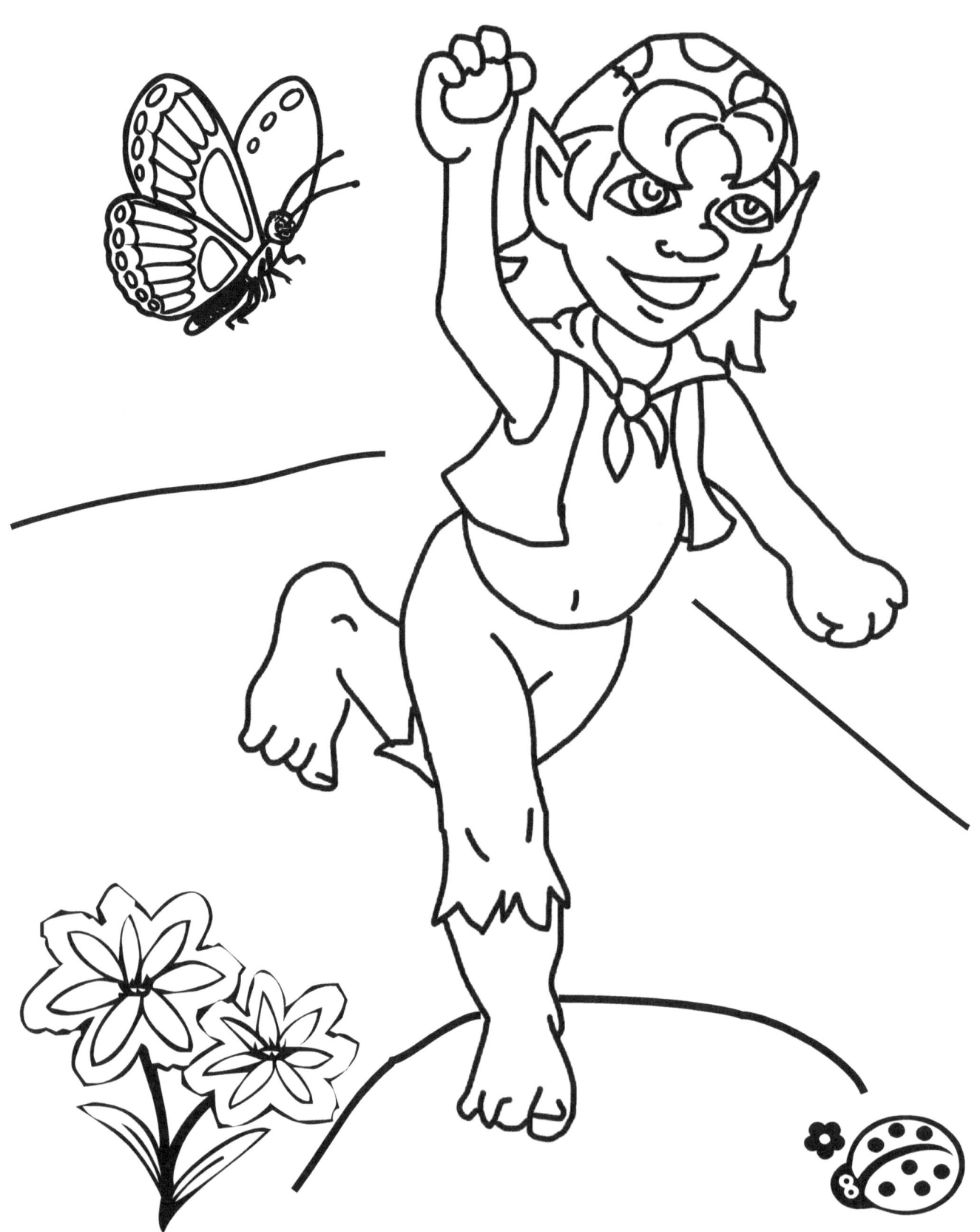

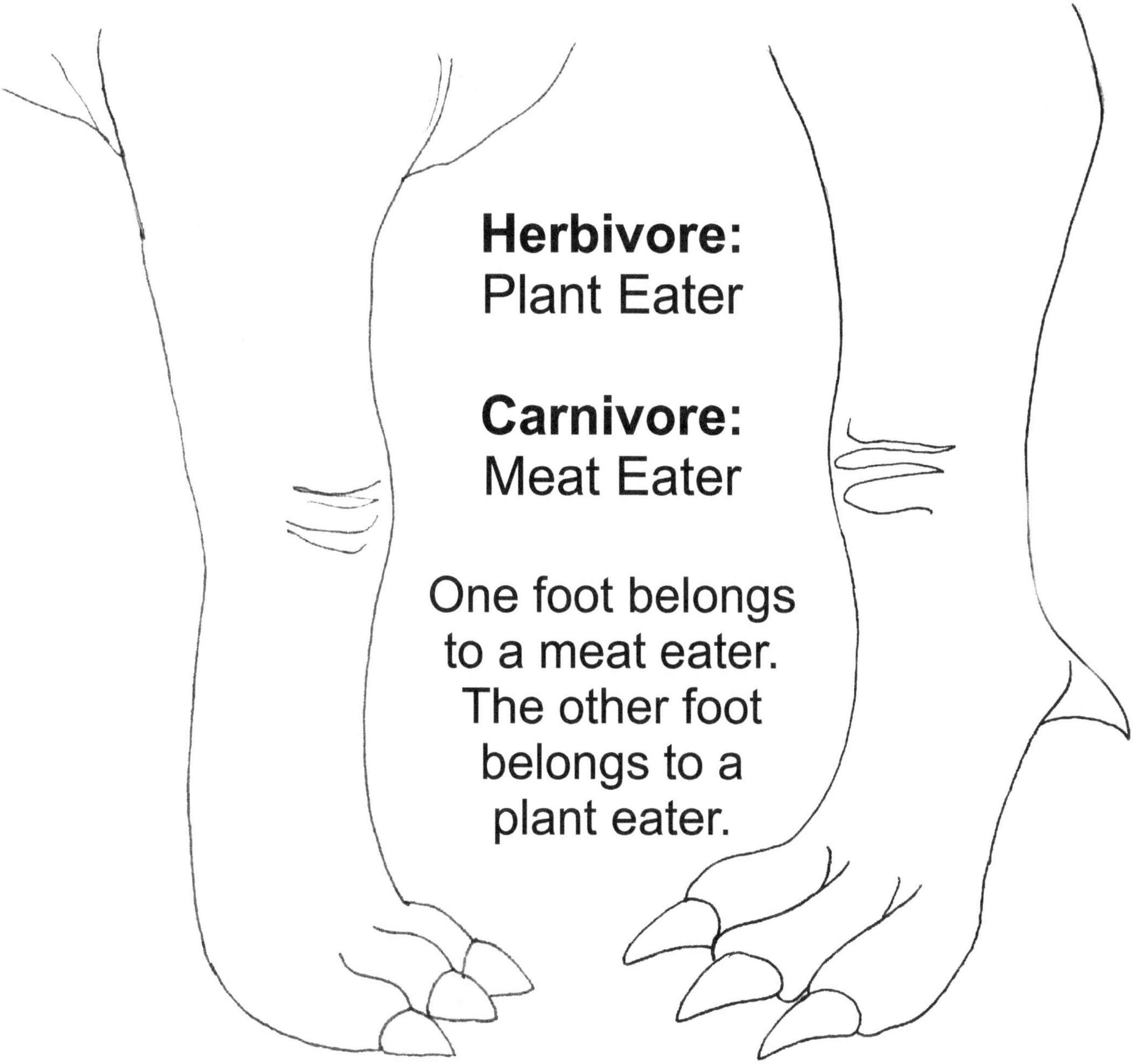

Herbivore:
Plant Eater

Carnivore:
Meat Eater

One foot belongs
to a meat eater.
The other foot
belongs to a
plant eater.

The baby dinosaur is a Herbivore.

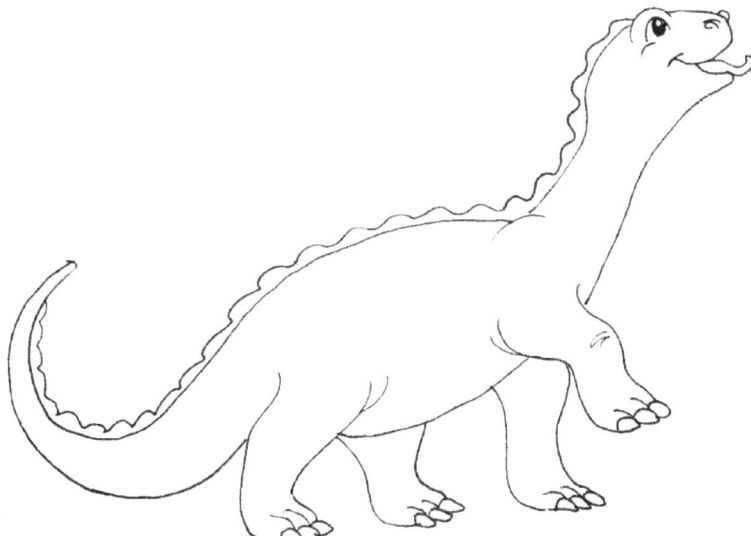

Can you color in
the leg that is the
baby's mother?

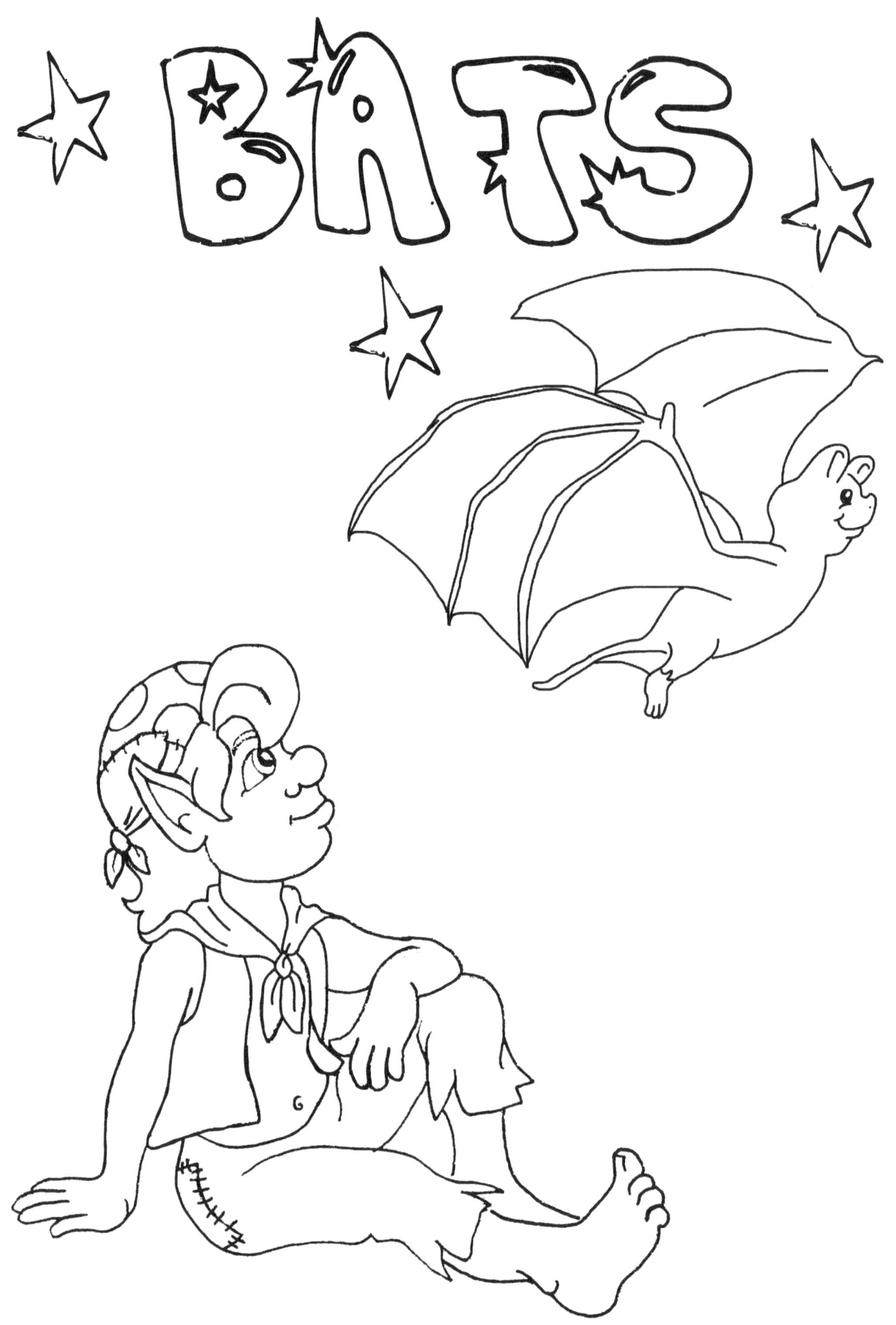

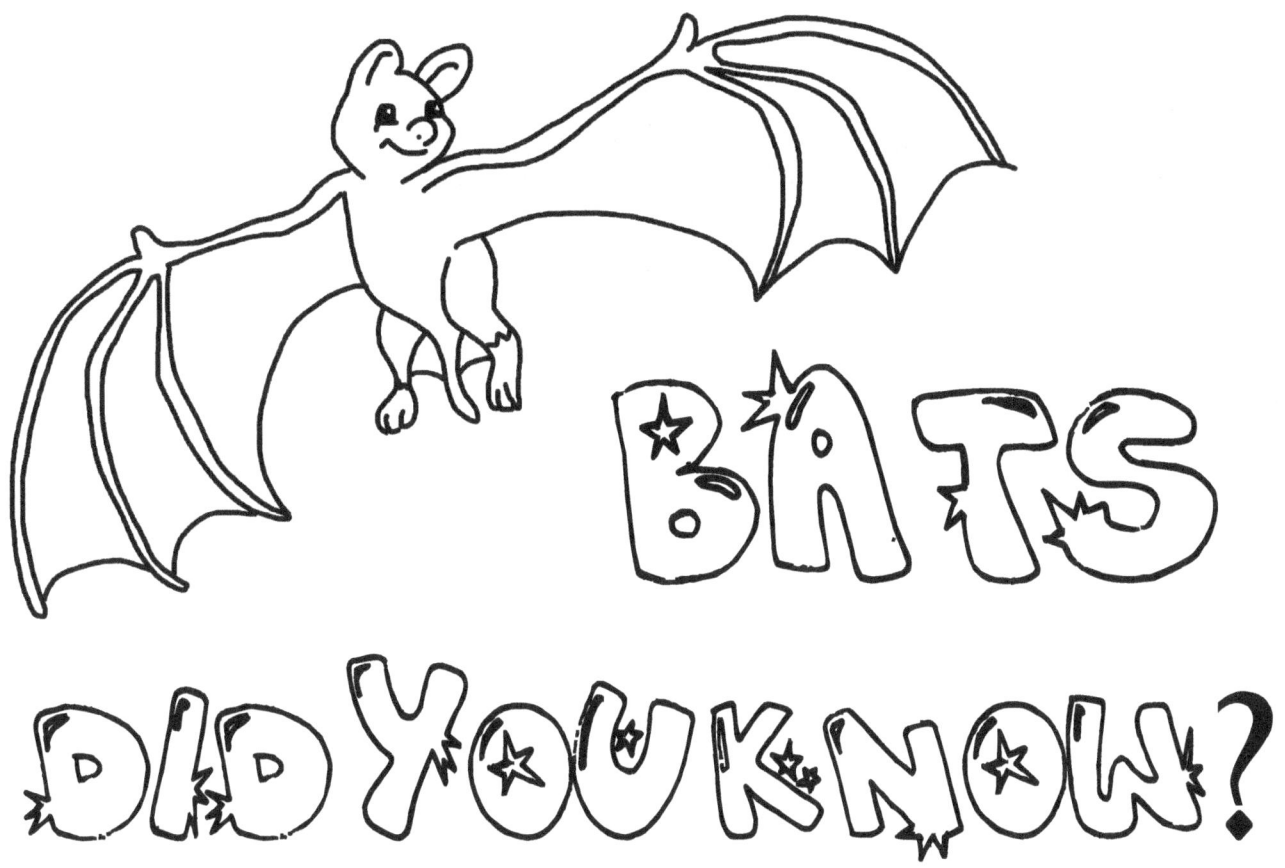

BATS

DID YOU KNOW?

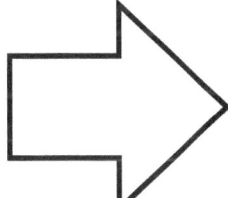 **Bats are nocturnal, meaning they mostly come out at night.**

Bats are the only mammals that can truly fly. A mammal is a warm-blooded animal. Birds are not mammals.

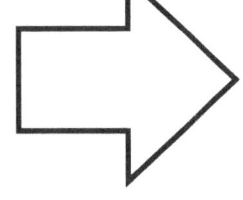 **Bats use Echolocation to fly. They use a series of beeps that echo off the walls and bounce back at them to "see" where to go. Most bats are blind.**

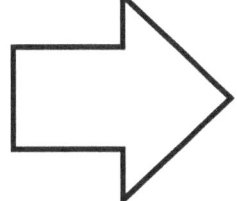 **There are 1100 species (types) of bats in the world. Some can be as small as 1 inch or as big as 5 feet long.**

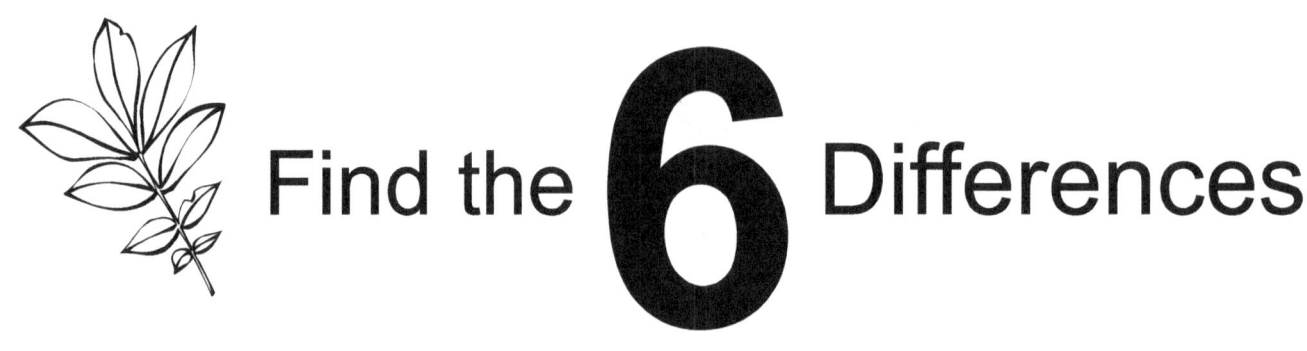

Find the **6** Differences

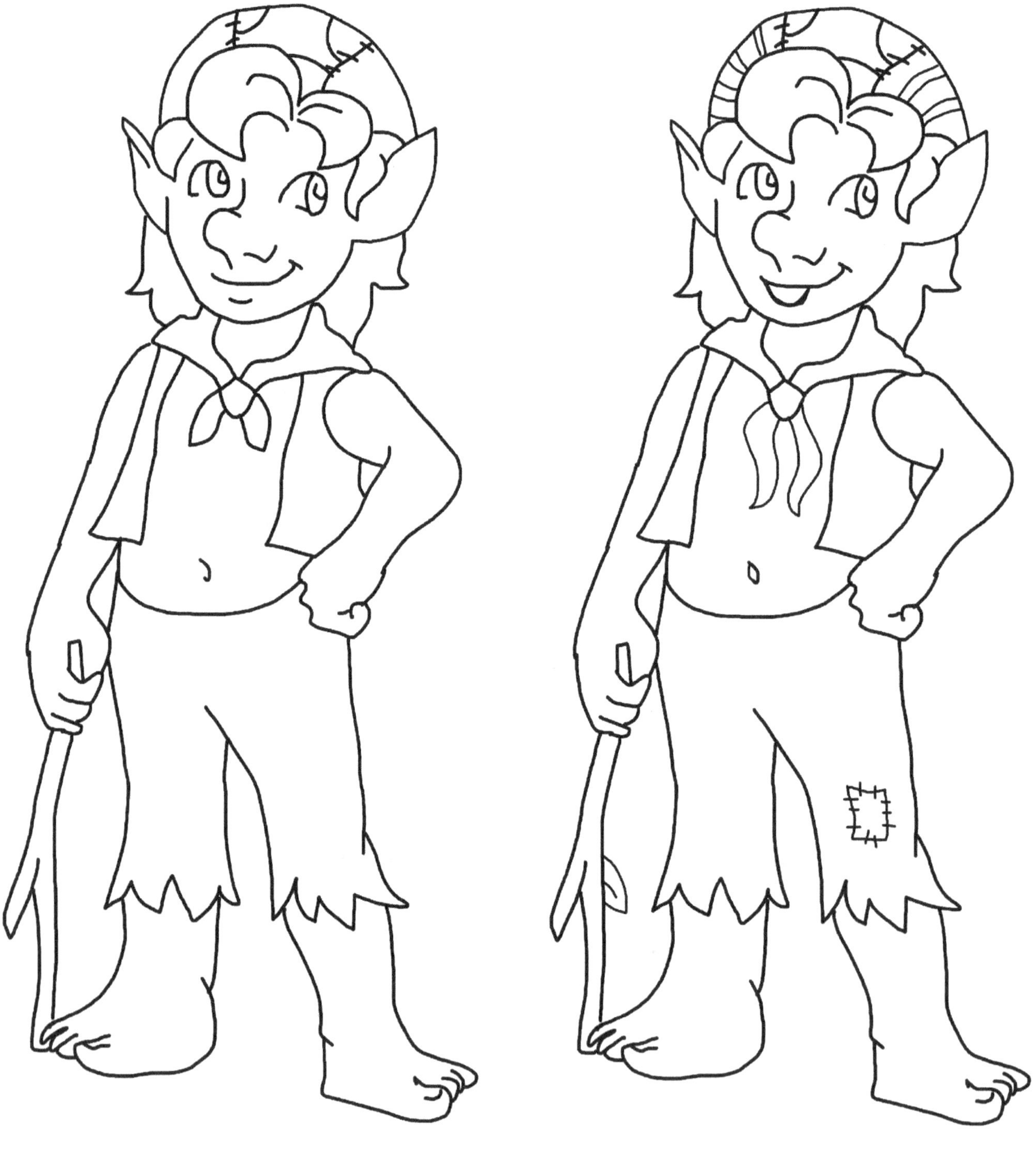

Circle the 6 differences on the Hamilton to the right.

Hhooooooooooooo

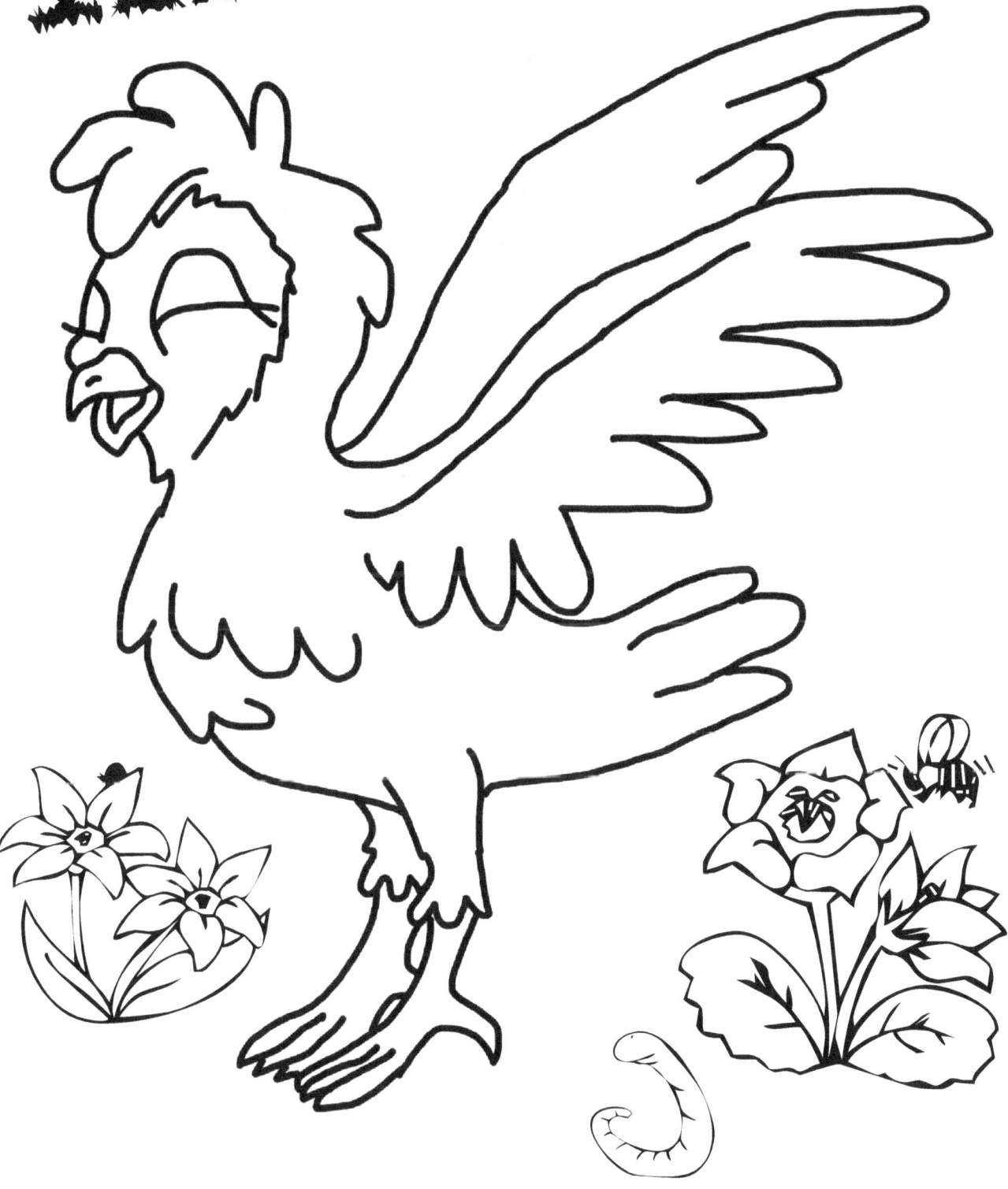

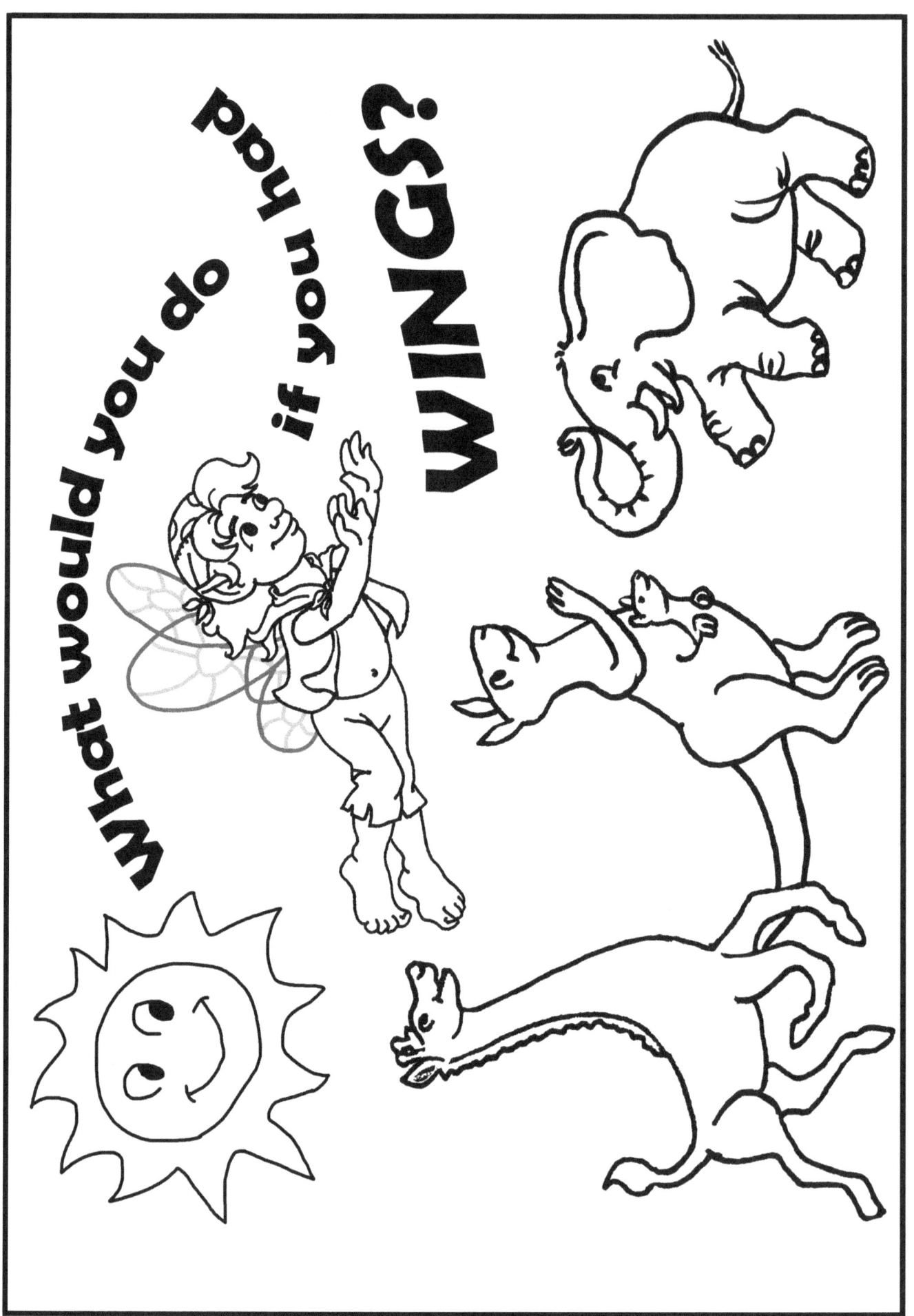

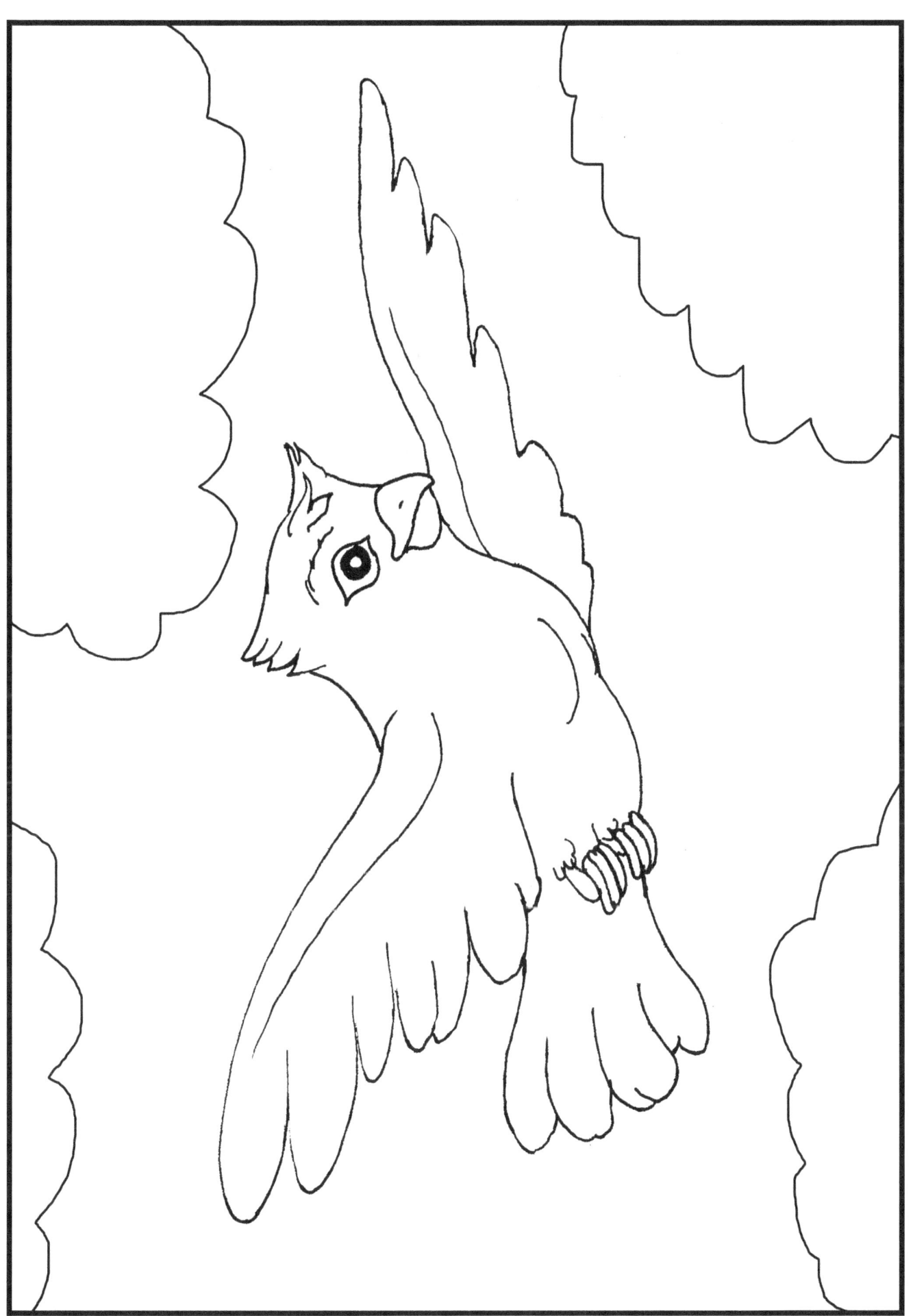

When the Wind Blows...

it makes it difficult for birds to fly. They get caught in wind currents which spiral them around. Help this bird make it through the wind currents to get to the other side.

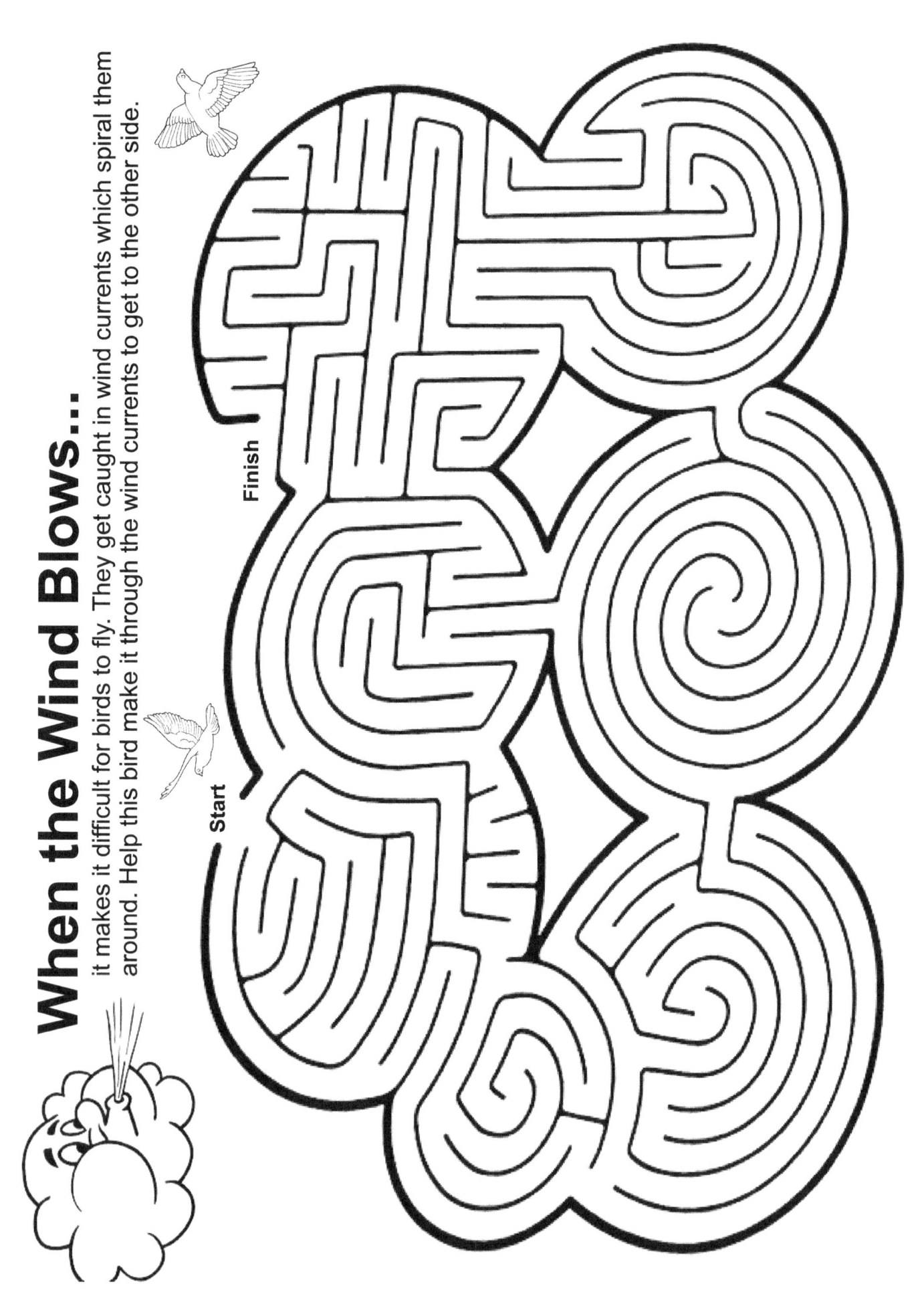

Finish

Start

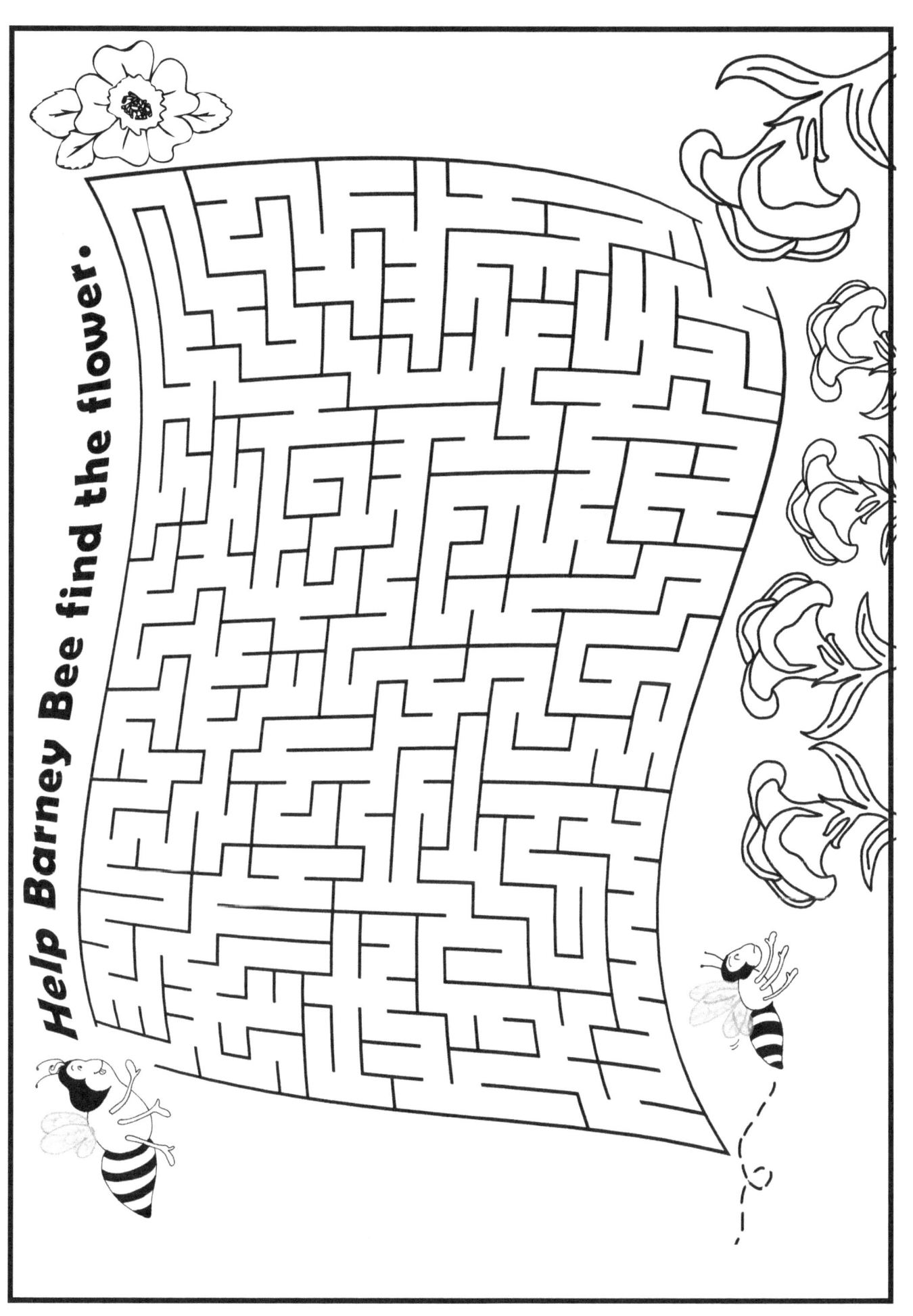

Help Barney Bee find the flower.

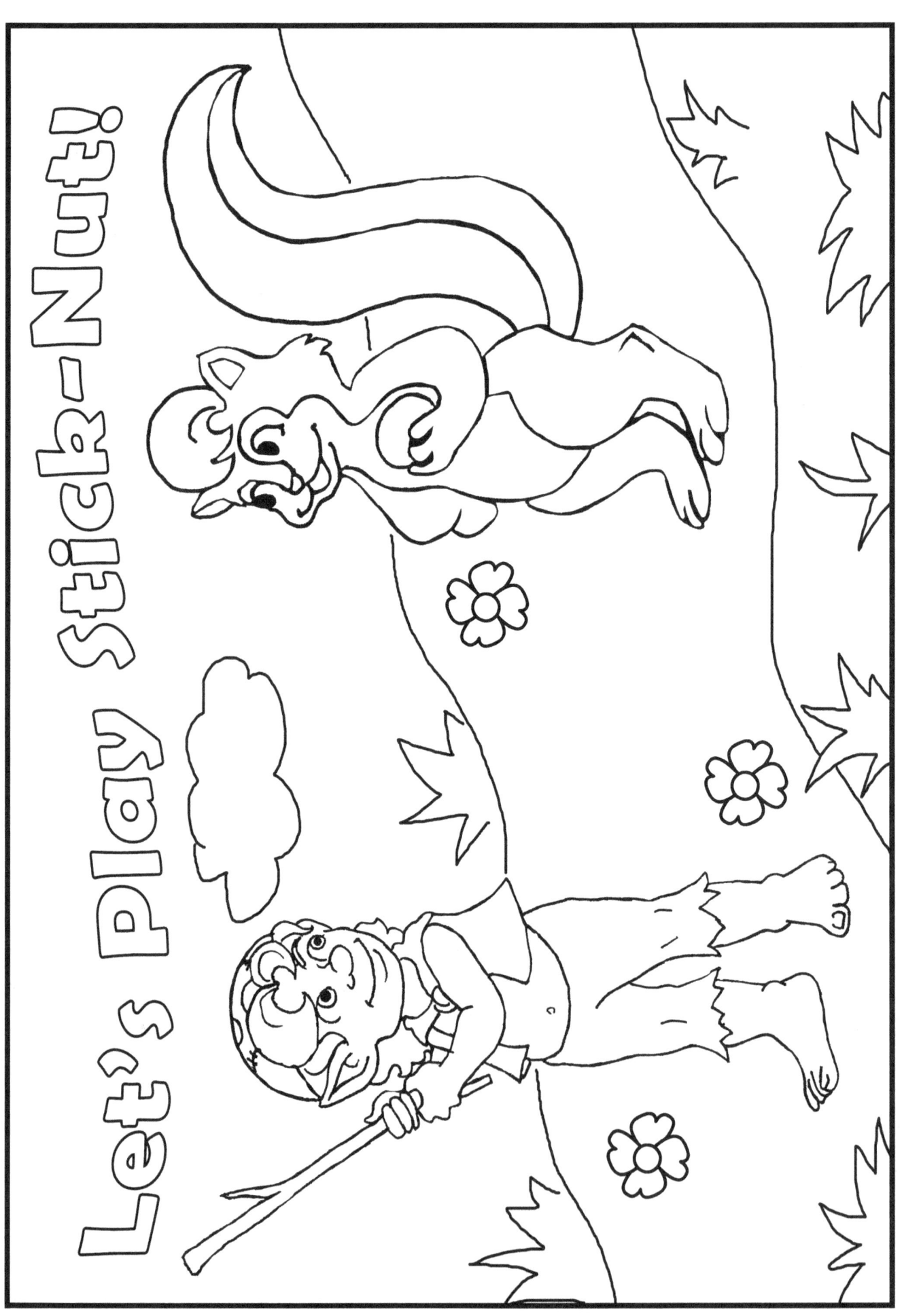

DID YOU KNOW?
STICK NUT

The game of 'stick nut' is similar to the human game of baseball. It is a fun, fast-paced game that anyone can play. Everyone who wants to play gets to play. They do not keep score, they just play until they are all tired. Everyone has fun.

The ball used is a hazel nut. Not only is this nut nearly spherical (round) but it tastes good too!

The bases are called dens, because if you are on home or in one of your dens, you are safe. If you are running between dens and get tagged by the nut you are out, but most of the time you make it back to home safely because everyone playing is all paws.

The stick can be any size or shape and many of the players choose their own sticks.

The pitcher is called the Nut Hurler or Nutter.

When a player hits the nut with the stick they run to the right base as fast as their little paws or wings can carry them.

CONNECT THE DOTS

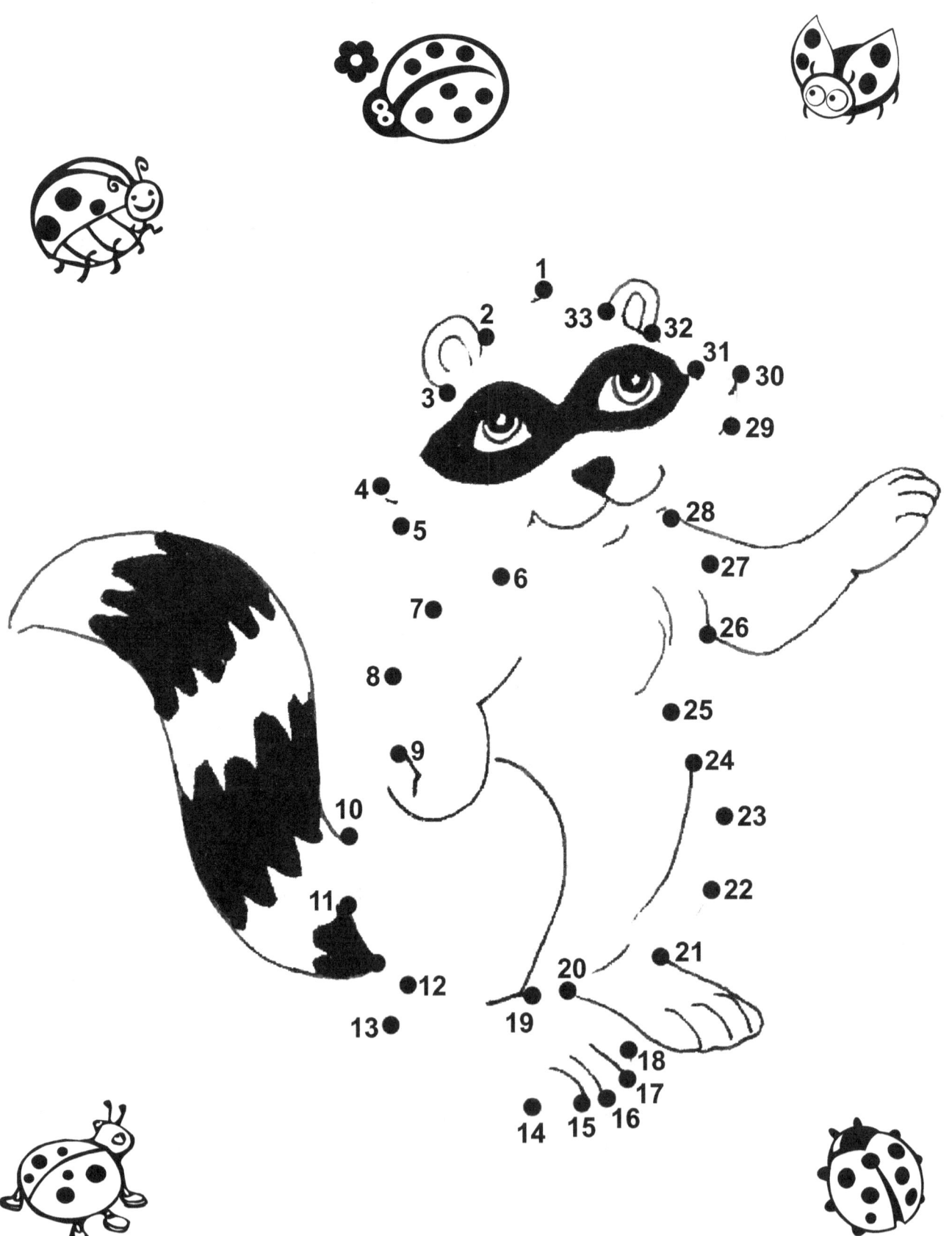

Help Pink Light Sprite find the perfect flower located in the center of this maze.

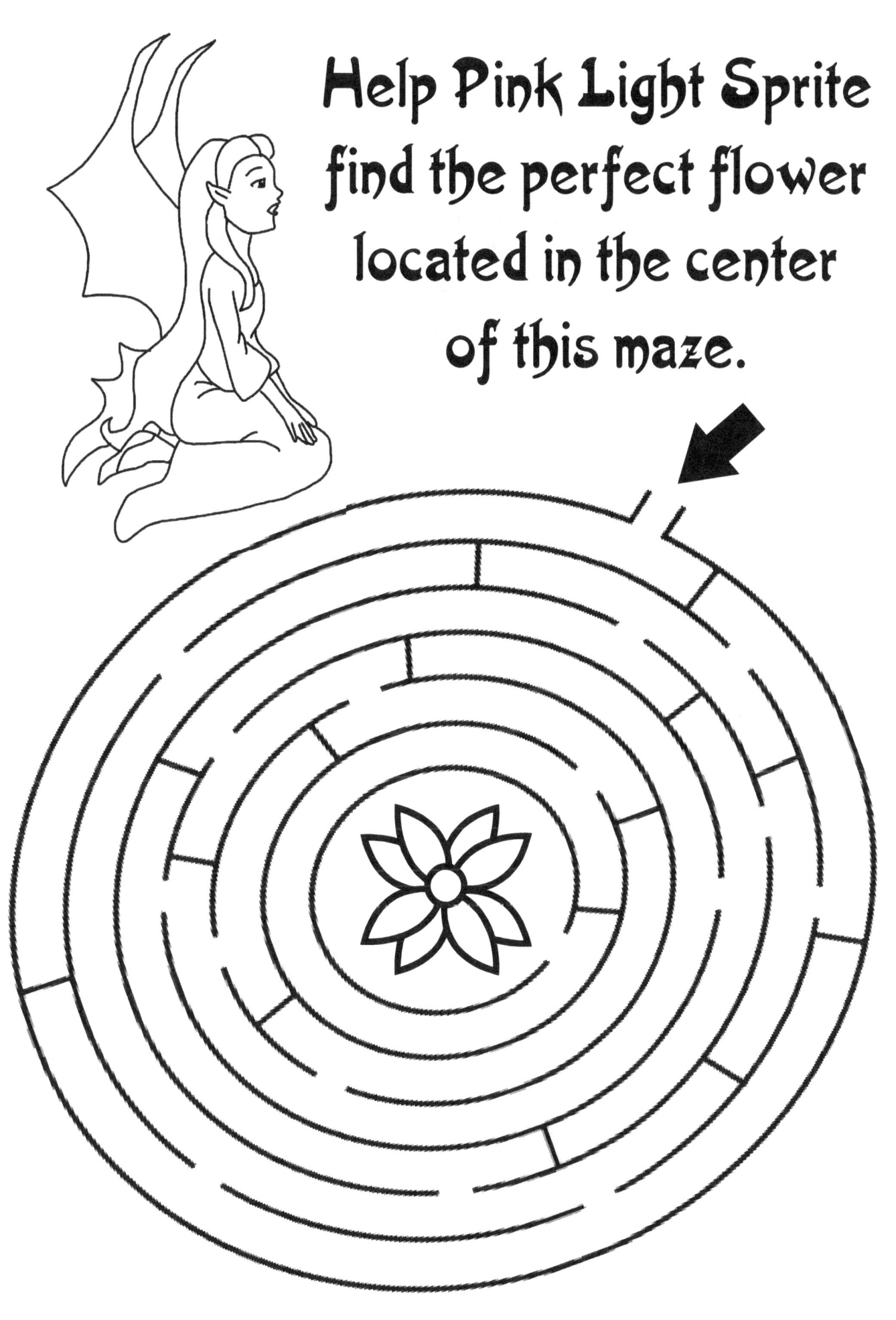

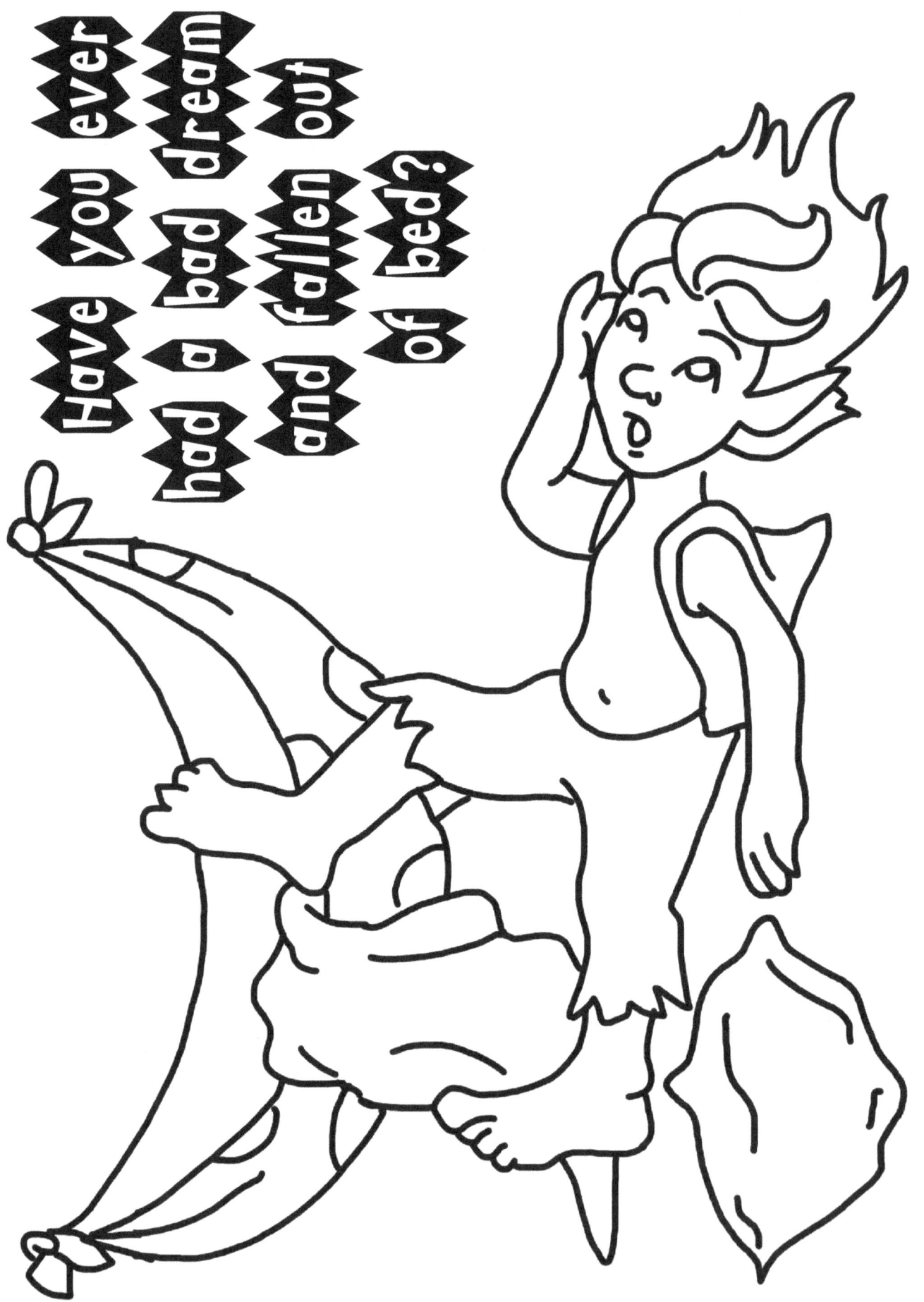

ALL AROUND:

Help Hamilton find the Snail.
Then Help the Snail find Hamilton.

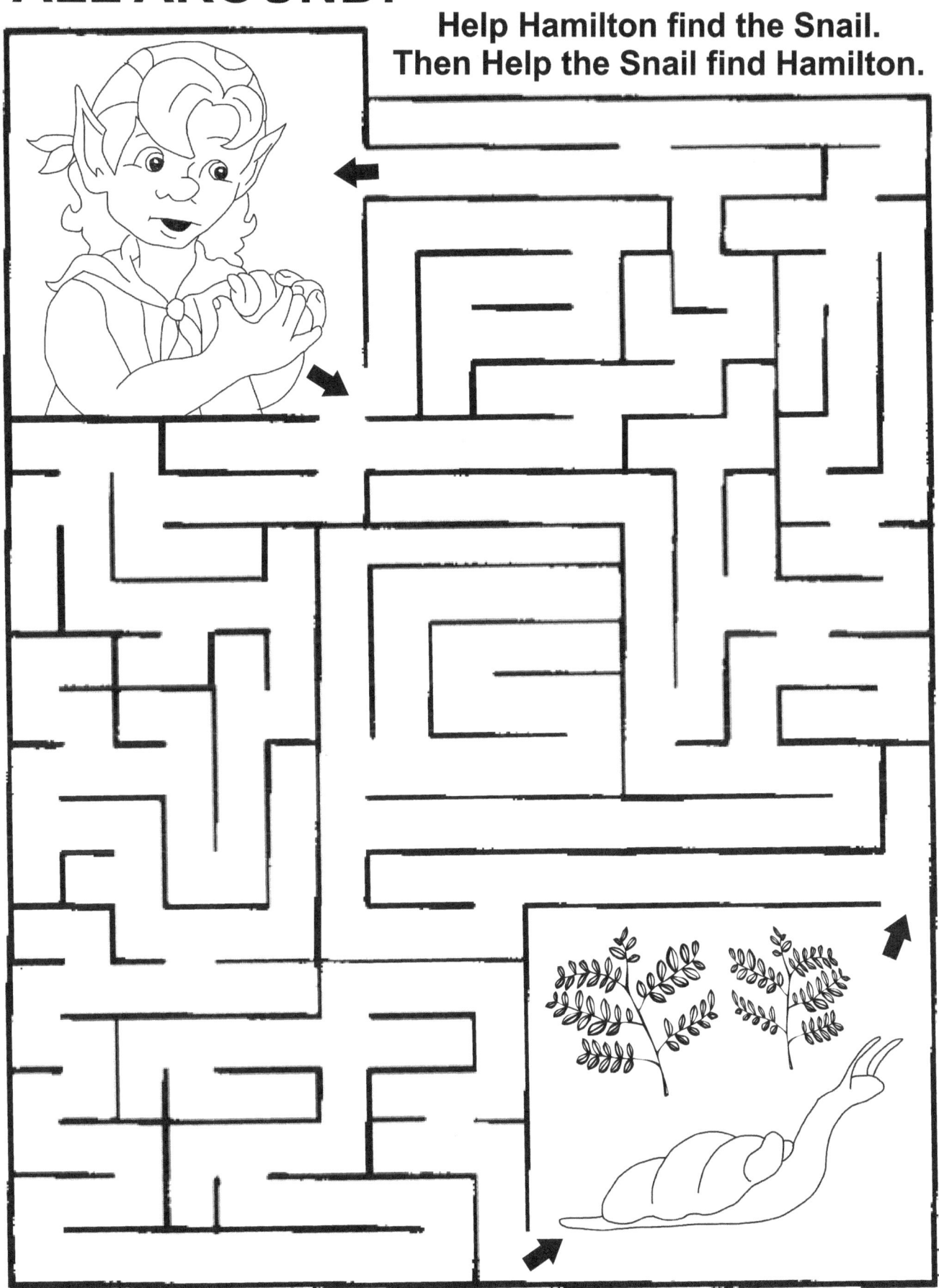

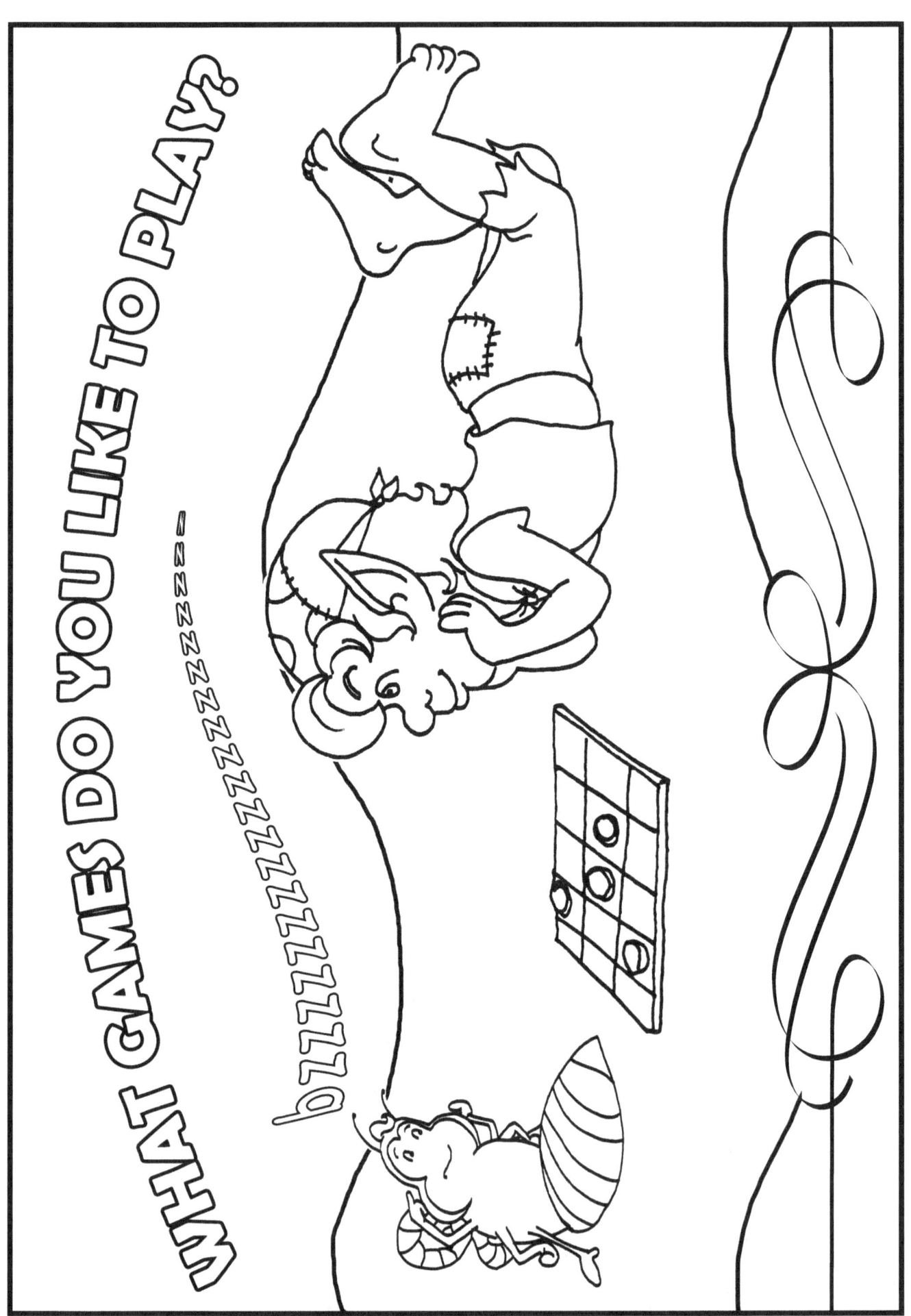

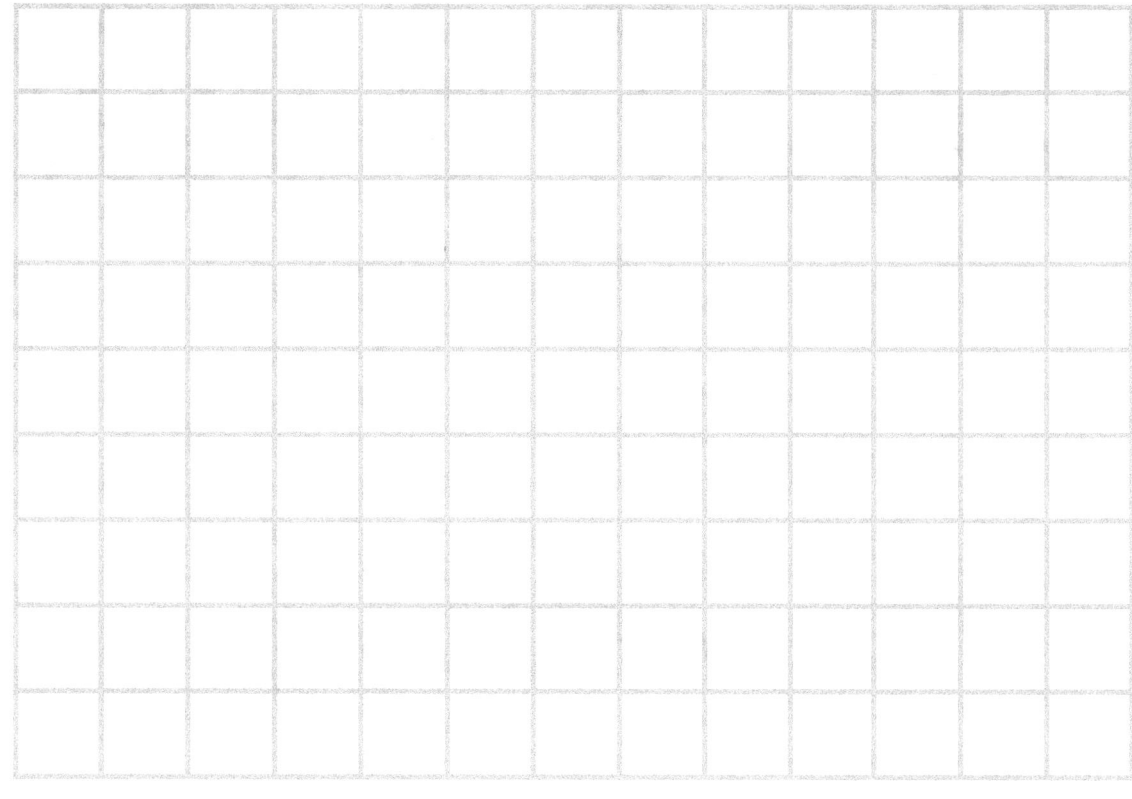

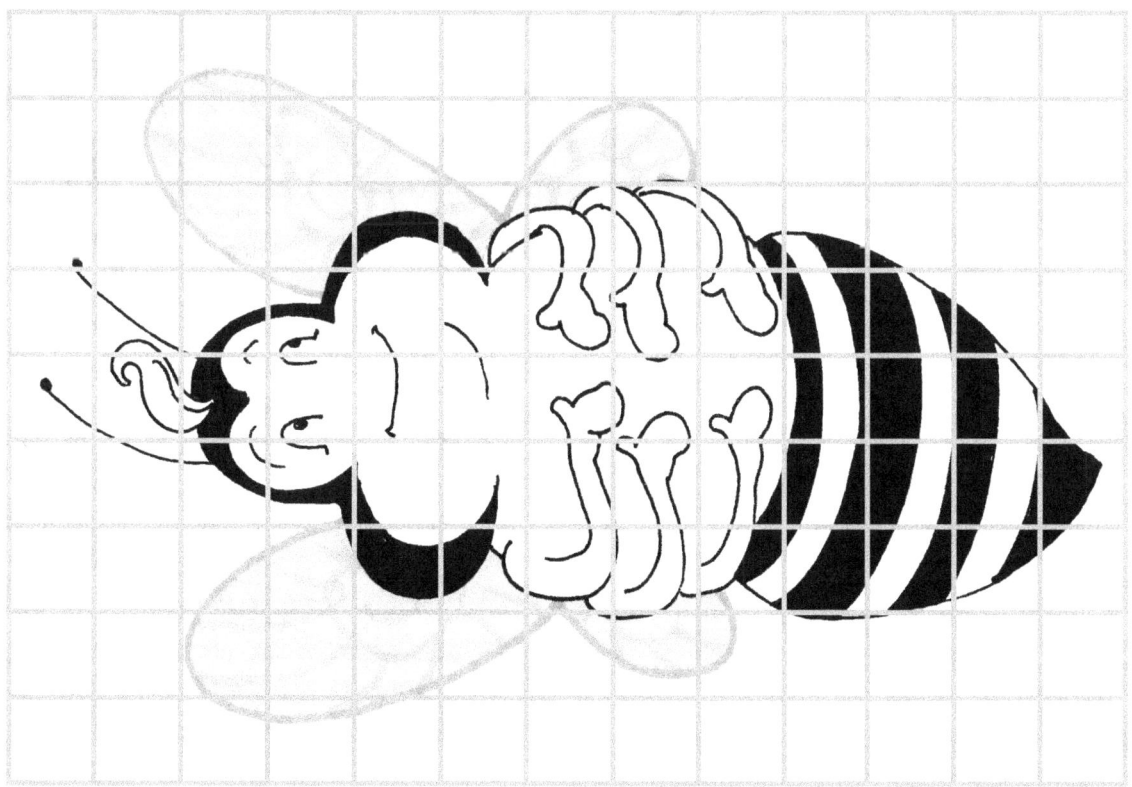

What is a Fossil?

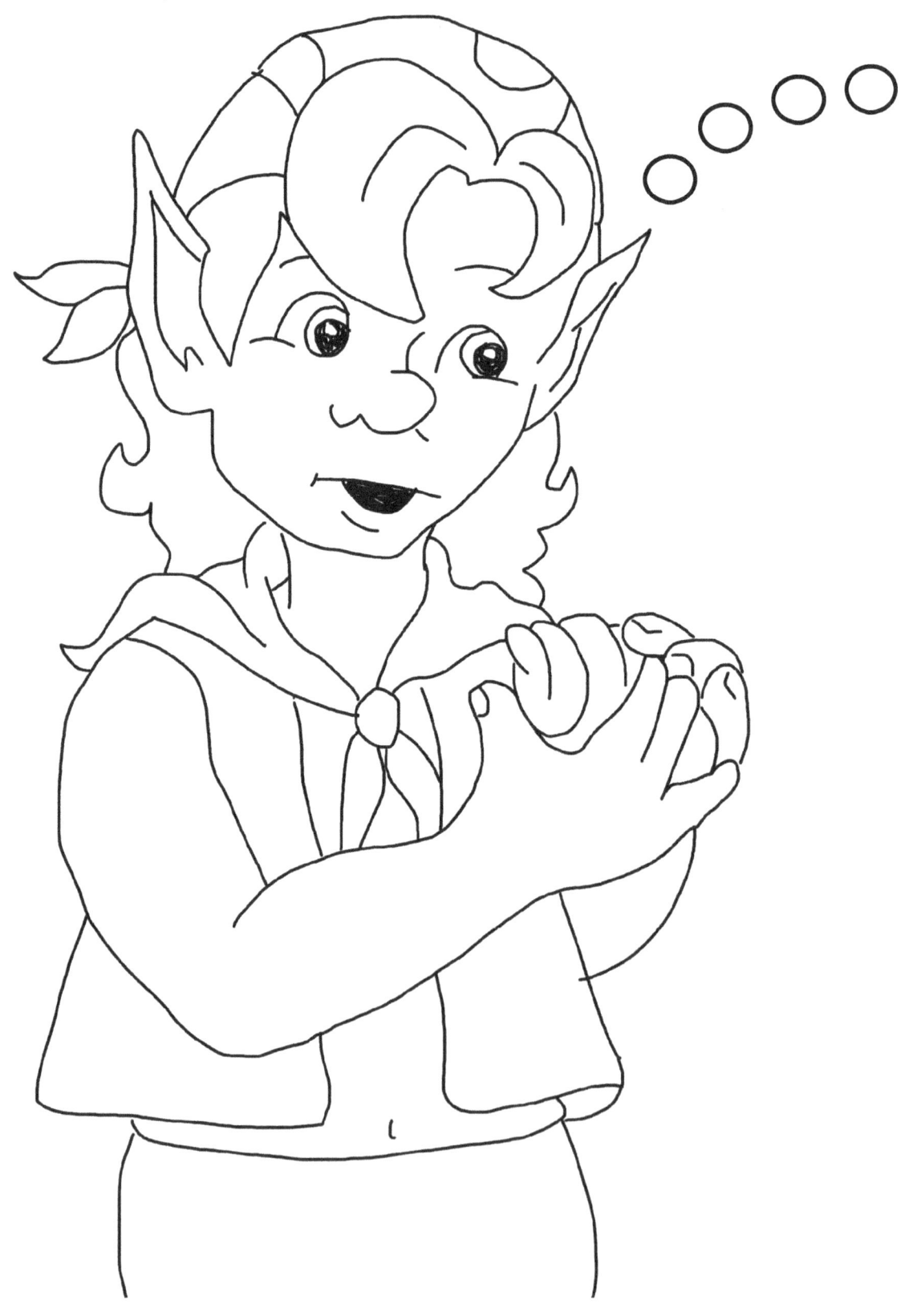

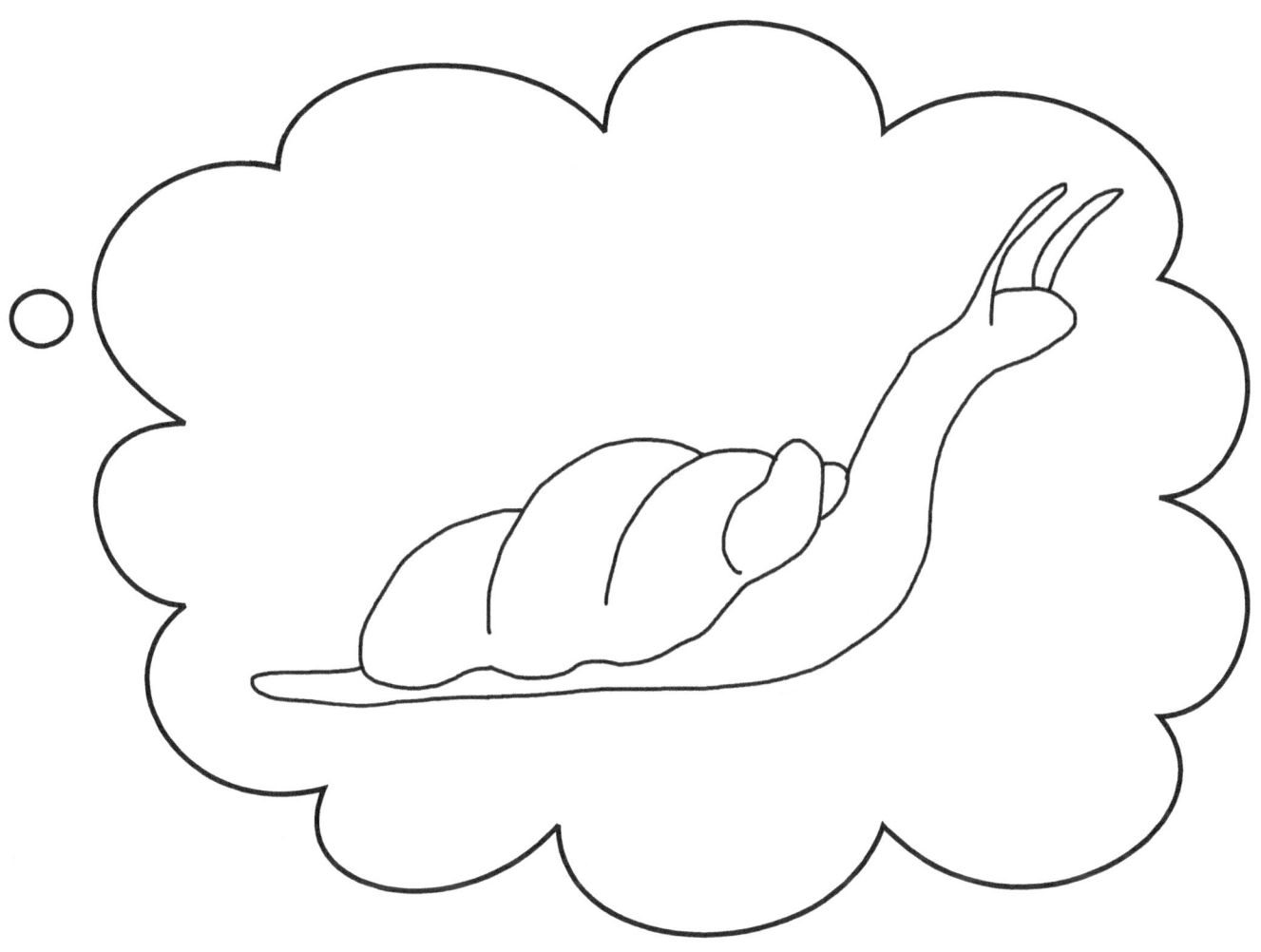

Fossil -

"Millions of years ago a snail came this way,
but at some point he died and his body decayed.
His shell filled with mud and soon went away
and what is left is this stone, that you hold today."
- Baxter Beaver

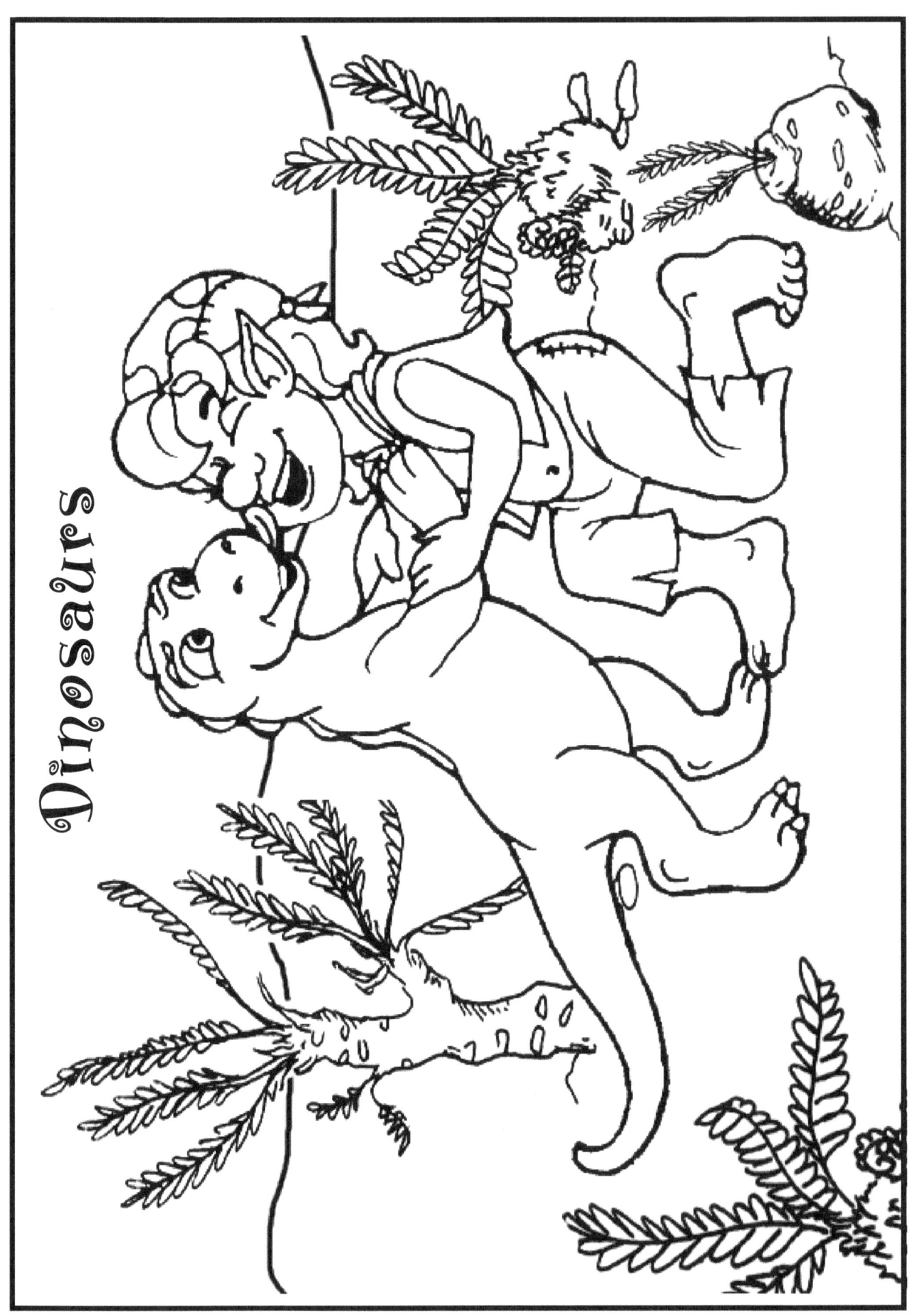

Dinosaurs

DID YOU KNOW?
Dinosaurs

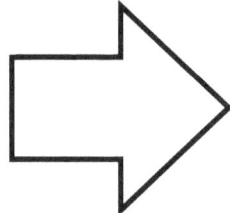 Dinosaurs lived 237 million years ago. They became extinct (all died out) 66 million years ago, so they lived on Earth for 171 million years.

237
-66
171

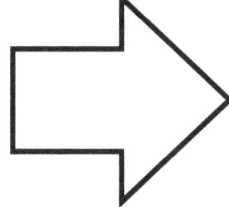 While dinosaurs became extinct, many species that lived along dinosaurs survived; like turtles, crocodiles, other reptiles, marine life and even birds.

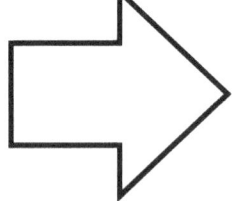 Dinosaurs were reptiles (cold-blooded) and laid eggs. Some dinosaurs were carnivorous (meat eaters) while others were herbivores (eating plants).

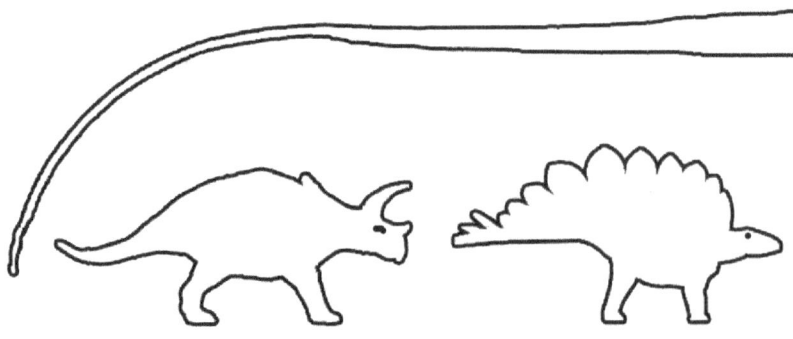

Dinosaurs

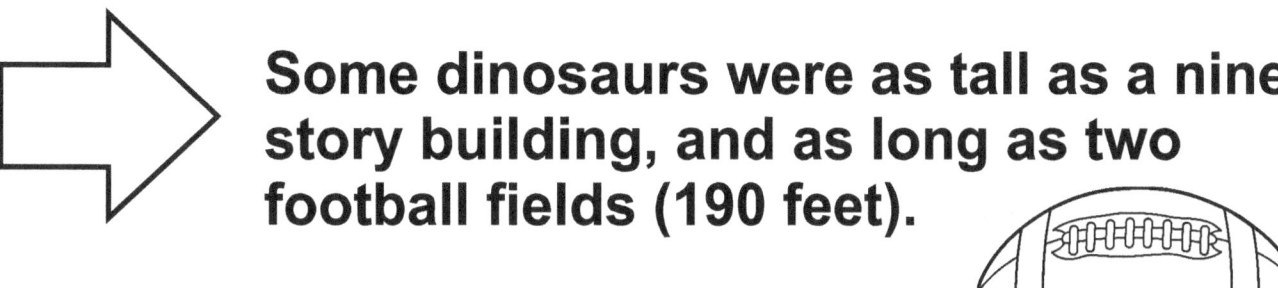

Some dinosaurs were as tall as a nine story building, and as long as two football fields (190 feet).

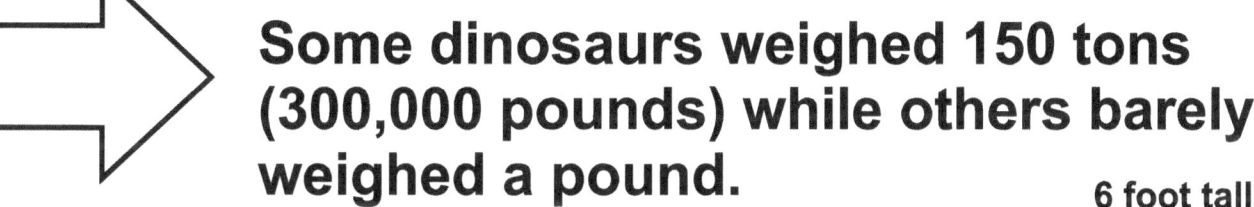

Some dinosaurs weighed 150 tons (300,000 pounds) while others barely weighed a pound.

6 foot tall human

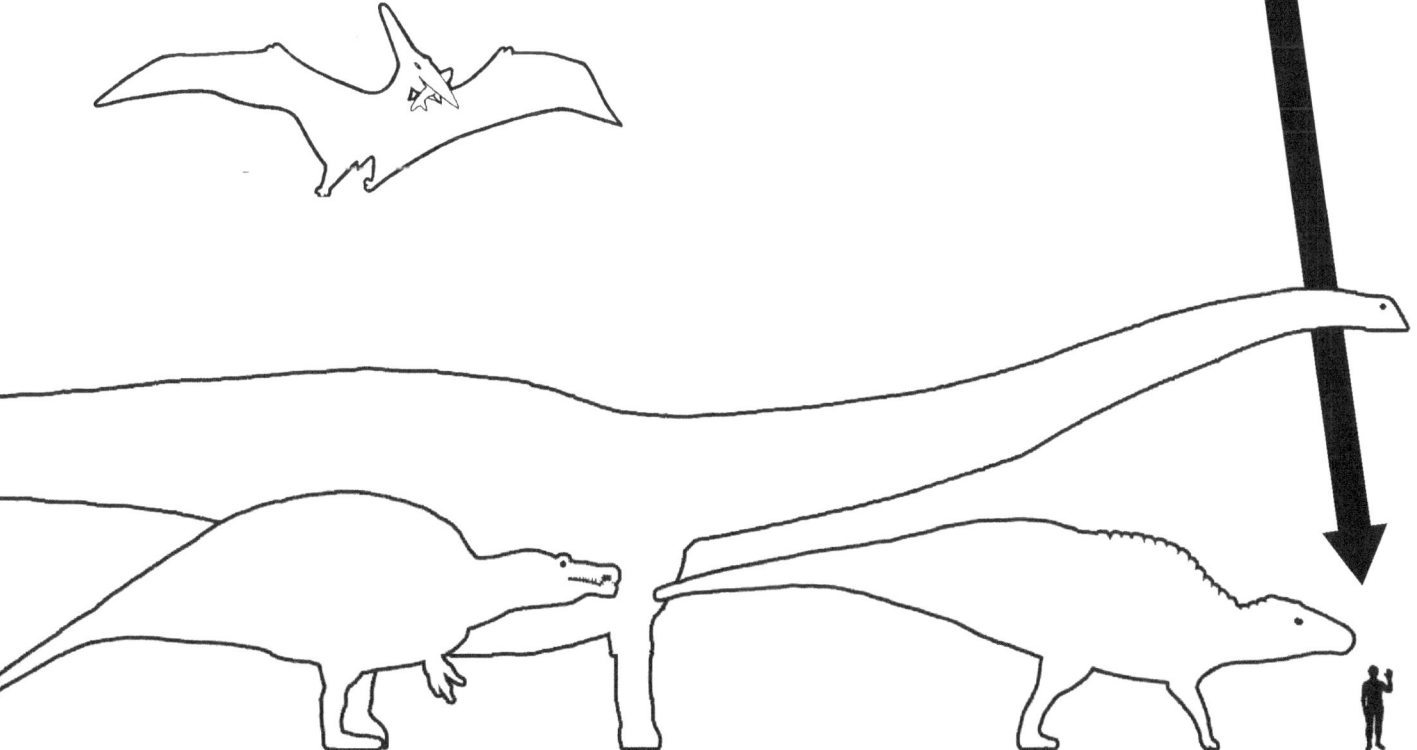

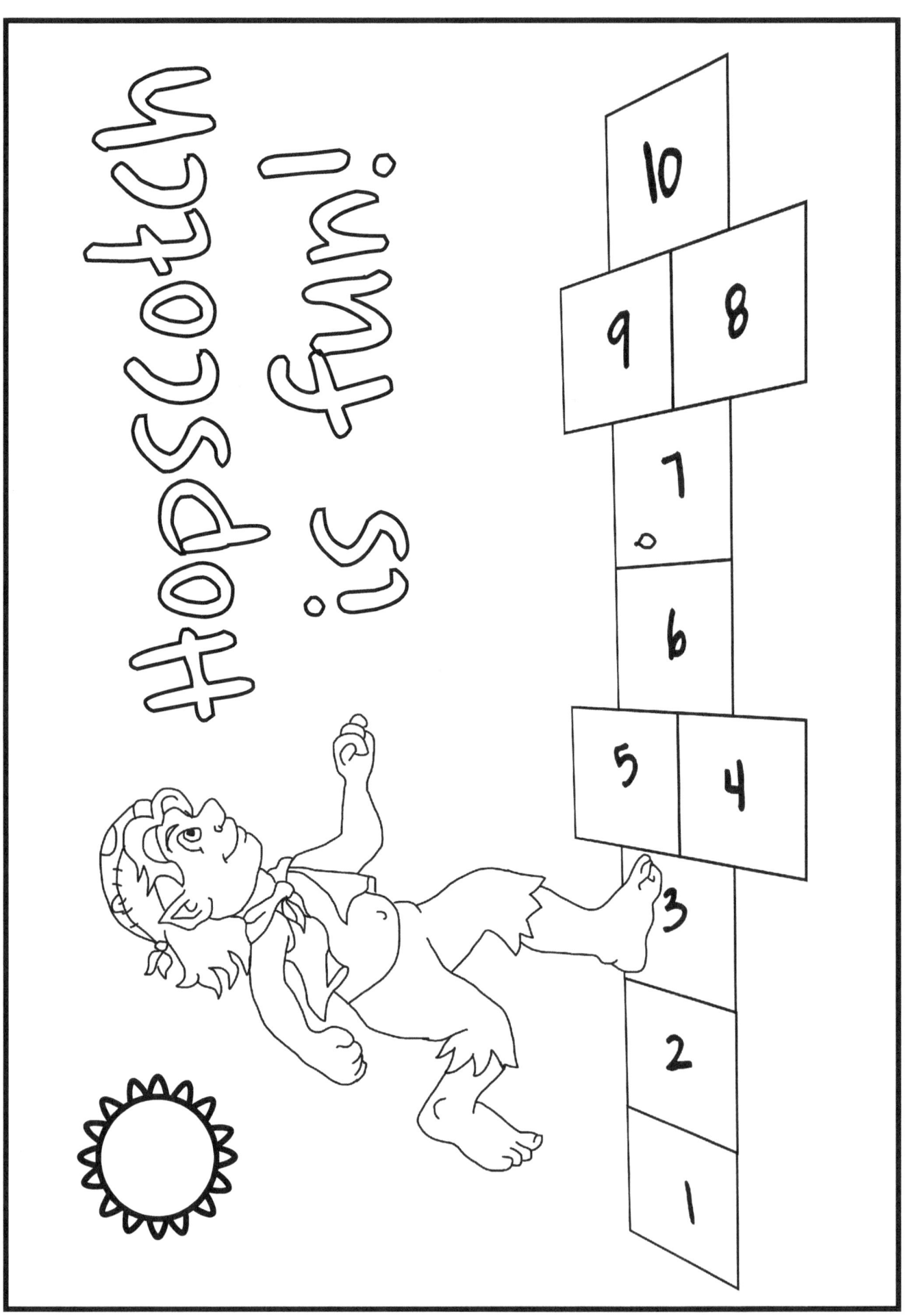

Hopscotch Rules:

1) Draw a grid on the ground either in the dirt with a stick or on the pavement with chalk.
   Make the grid as easy or hard as you want.
   You can even make up things that can be done in the grid; like going different directions.
2) Throw a marker: rock, coin or small toy, to the first square.
   This is the square you will hop over.
3) Single squares must be hopped onto with one foot.
   Double squares both feet (one foot on each square).
4) When you get to the last square, turn and come back down, retrieving the marker.
   Don't land on a line or your turn ends.
5) If you made it all the way back without landing on a line, you can continue your turn,
   throwing the marker into the 2nd square and repeating these steps.
6) Whoever gets all the way to the end wins.
7) Or make up your own rules. Be creative and imaginative! Have fun!

Optional Designs:

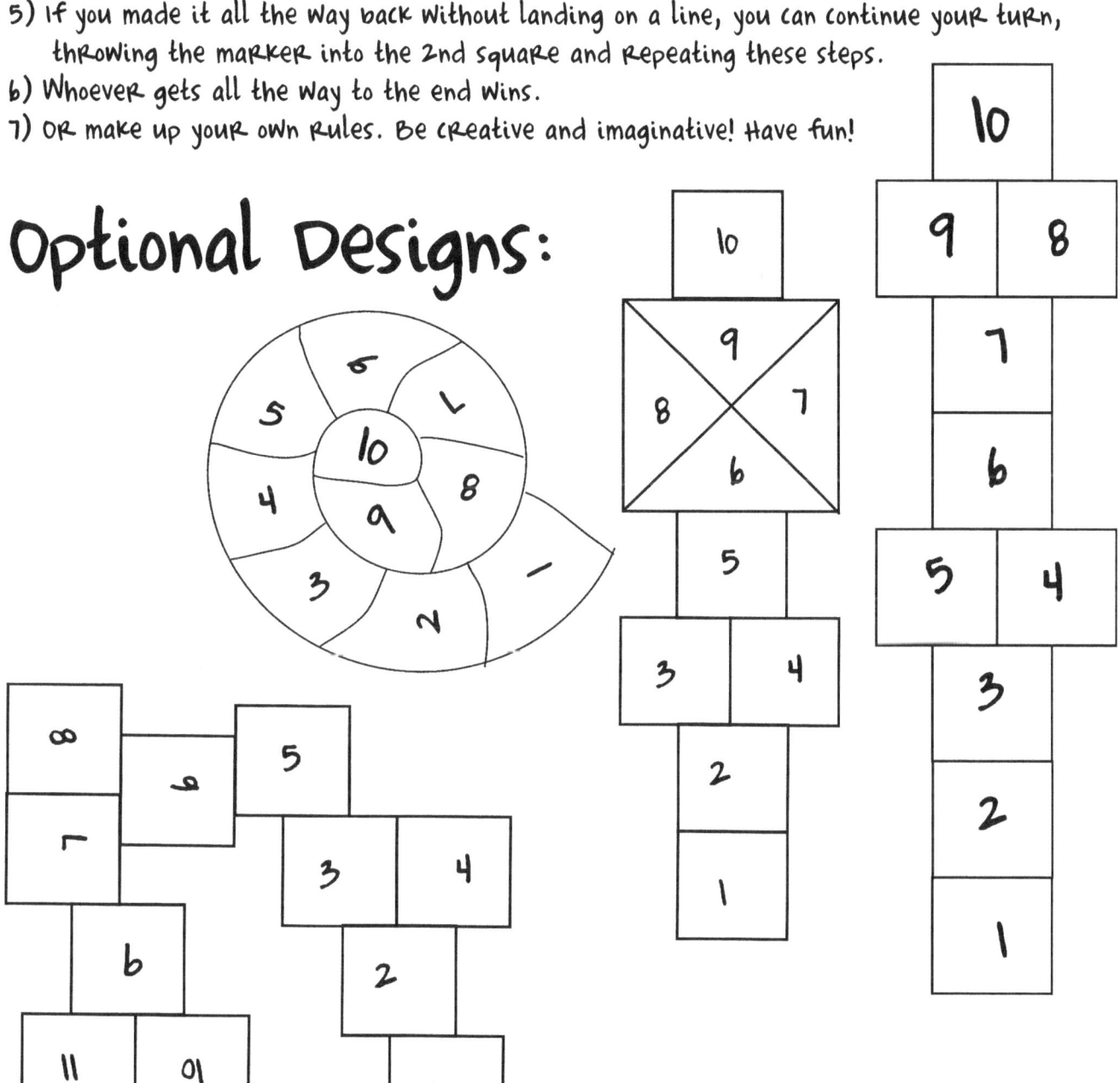

You may come up with other designs.

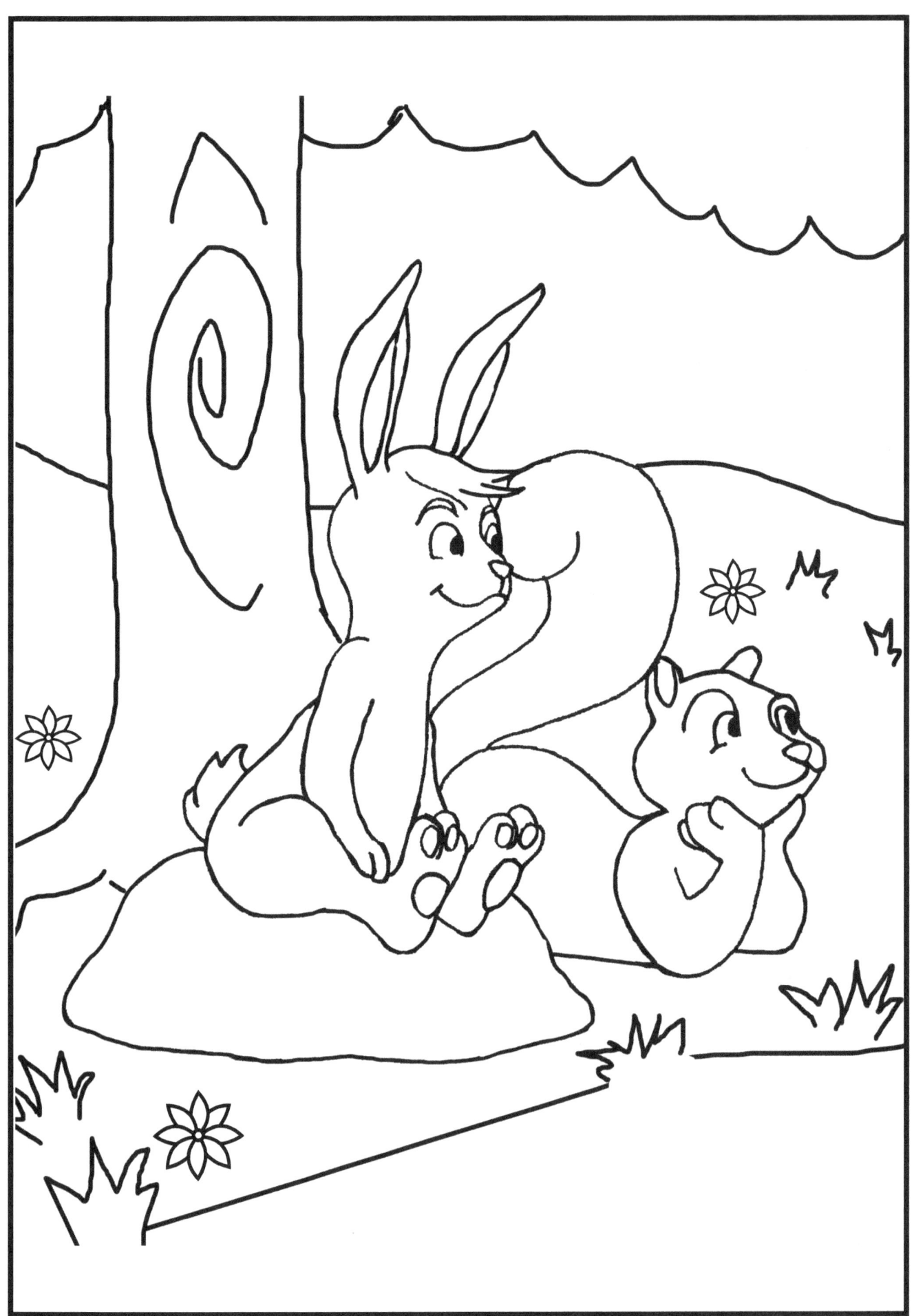

WORD SCRAMBLE

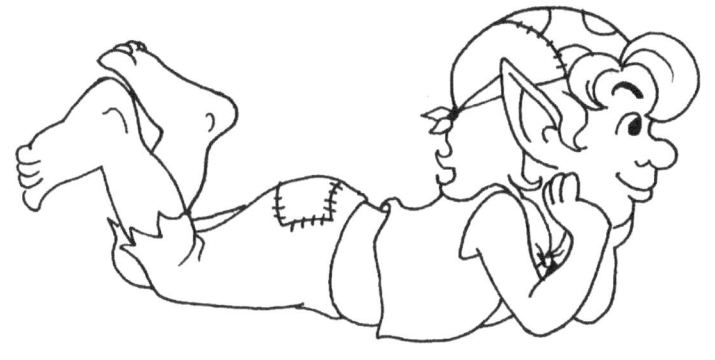

The letters are all mixed up but when put in the right order will spell the names of the story book characters.
Fill in the spots on the right.
Use the word bank in the bottom box for help.

KNIP TILGH TEPRIS

YEBRAN EBE

AAARM LODIMRALA

KWTIAHRE LOW

ELRME SOUME

DELOOW

REKETSE KKSUN

NILTAHOM LORTL

RTTTEOACNH

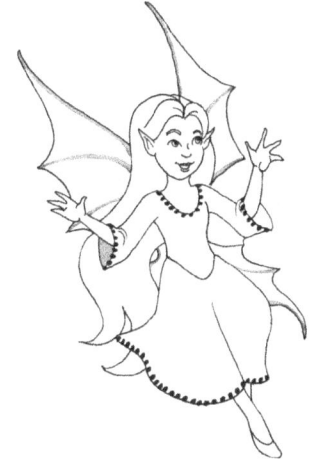

WORD BANK

AMARA ARMADILLO   BARNEY BEE
CHATTERTON   ELWOOD
HAMILTON TROLL   MERLE MOUSE
SKEETER SKUNK   WHITAKER OWL
PINK LIGHT SPRITE

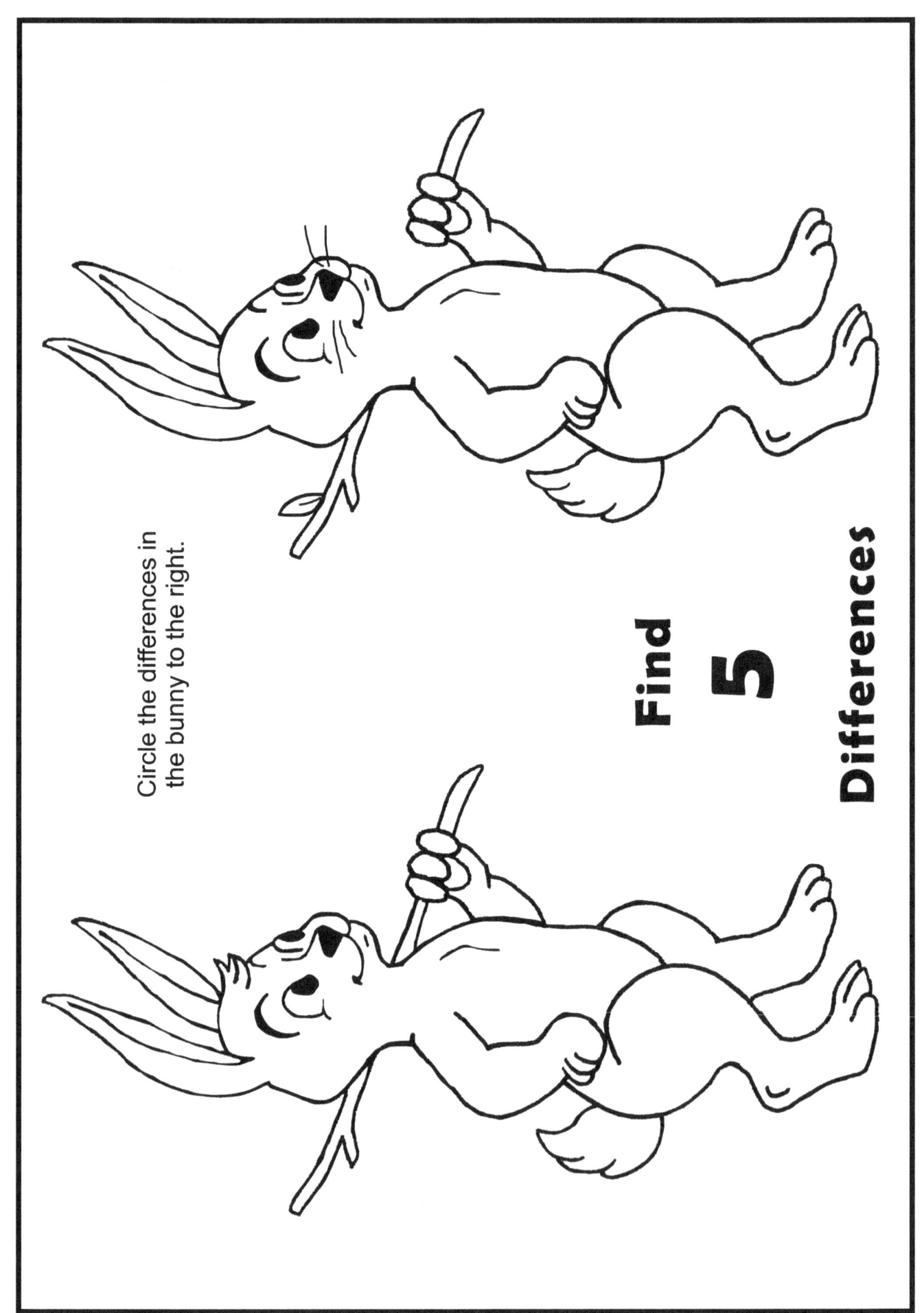

Circle the differences in the bunny to the right.

Find

5

Differences

HELP HAMILTON TROLL FIND HIS HOME

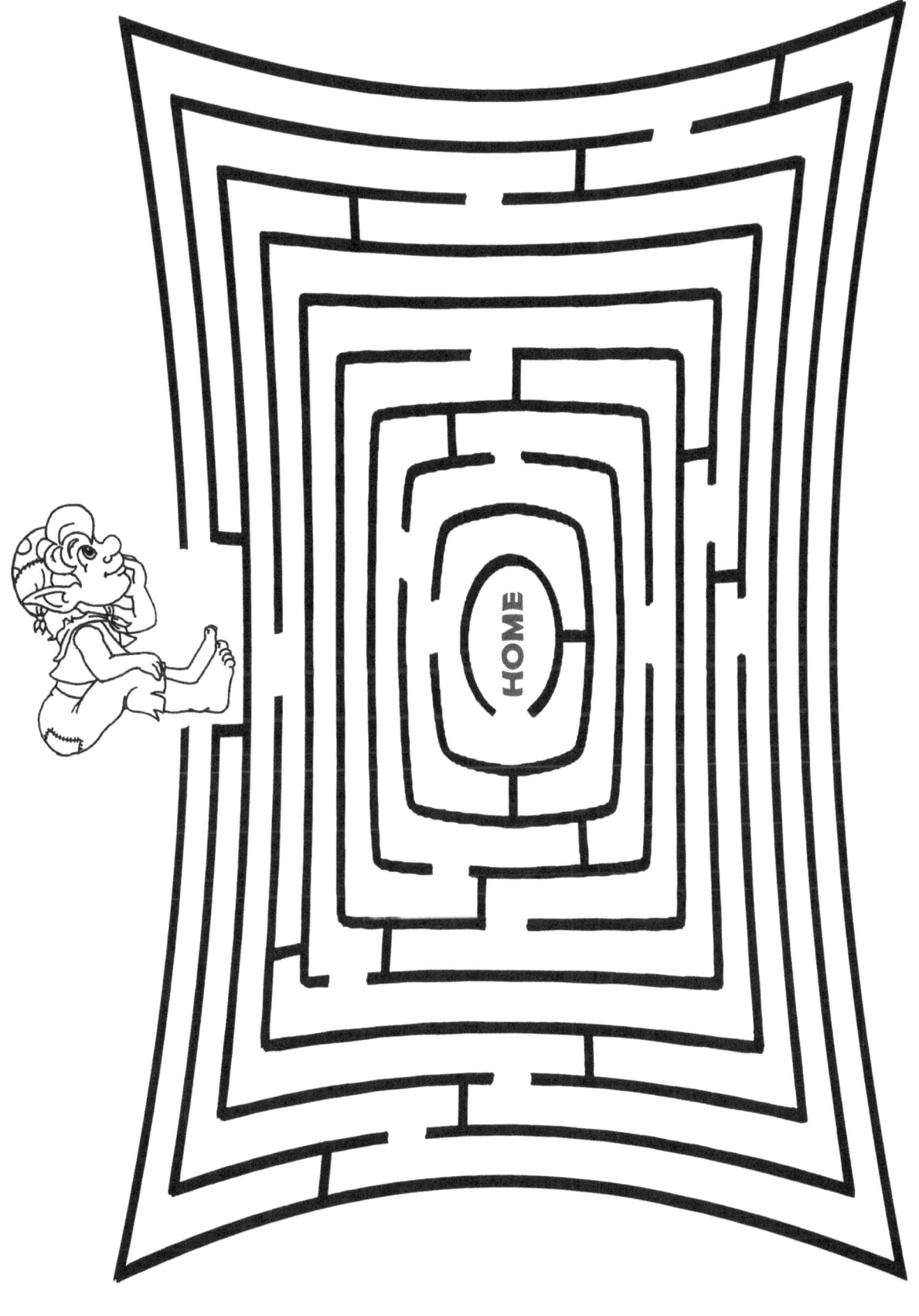

CROSSWORD PUZZLE

ACROSS

1. THE SIGN IS CALLED HIDE AWAY ____

2. BARNEY BEE LOVES ____

3. THE GAME THEY PLAY IS ____

4. WHITAKER OWL LEARNS TO ____

5. CHATTERTON IS A ____

DOWN

1. THE LEAVES MAKE
   THE SHAPE OF A ____

2. PINK LIGHT ____

3. HAMILTON IS A ____

Which worm will Elwood get?

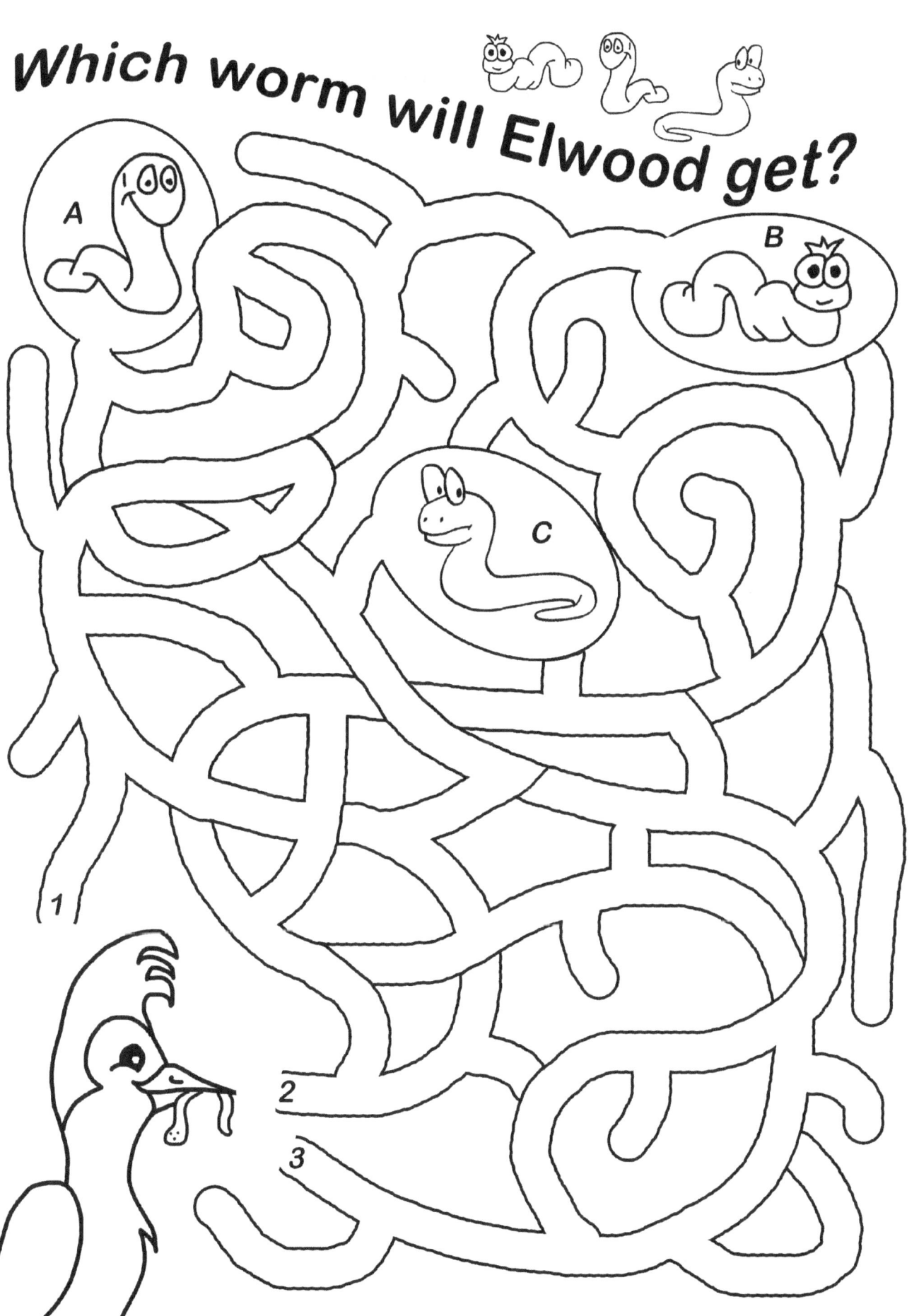

Which Squirrel is NOT like the others?

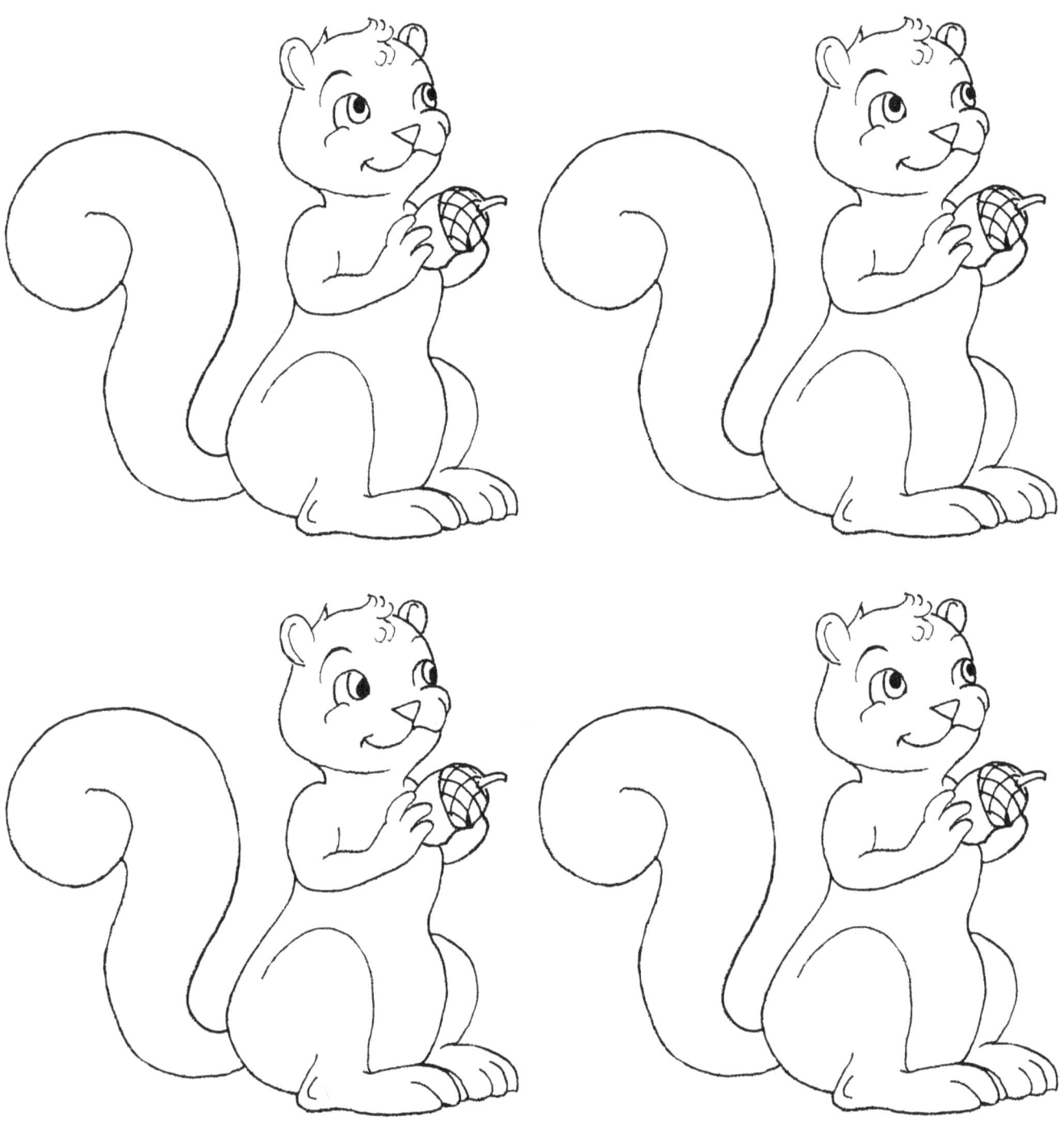

One of these squirrels has something different about them. Find which one it is and circle it.

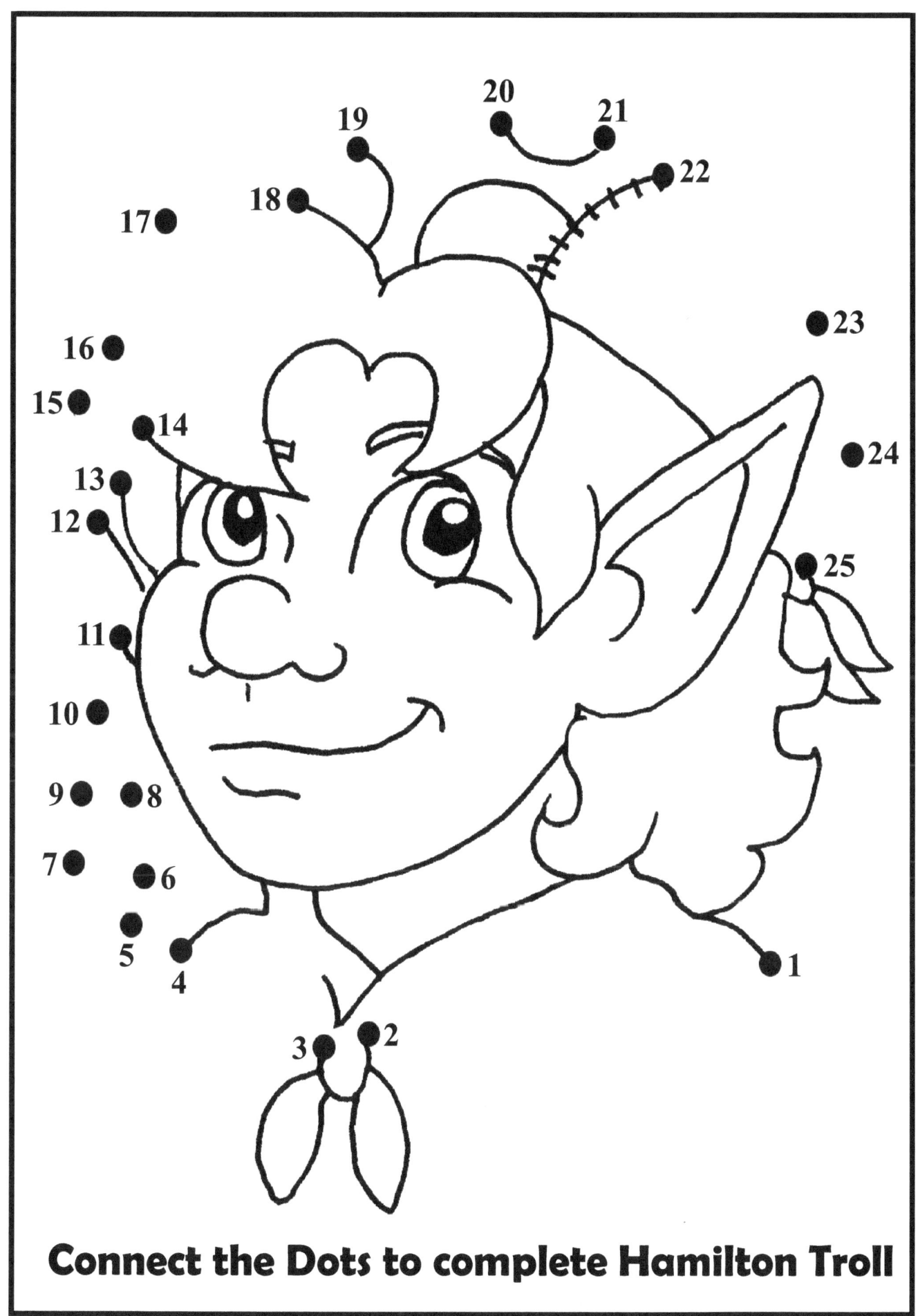

Connect the Dots to complete Hamilton Troll

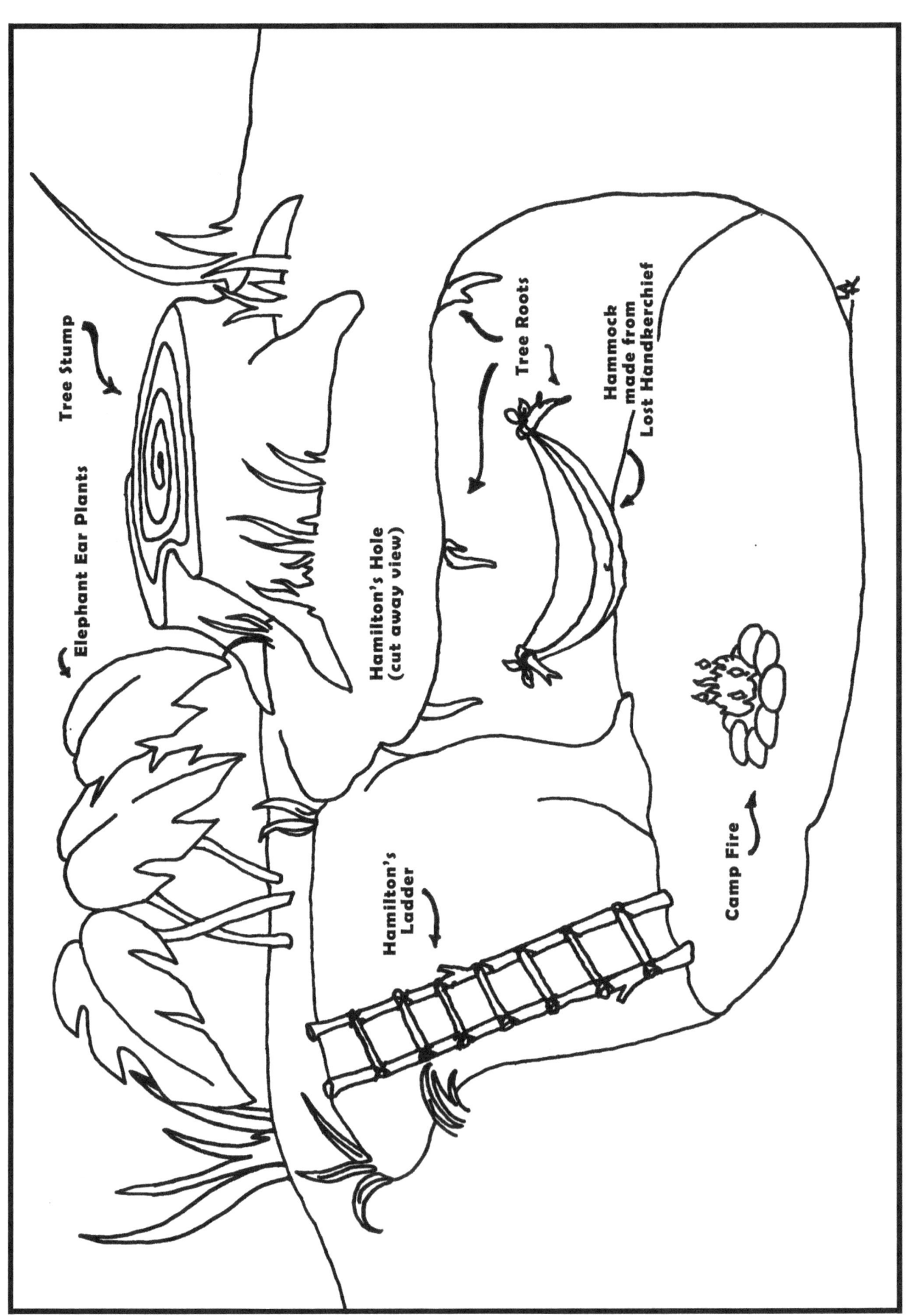

Learn to DRAW Hamilton Troll

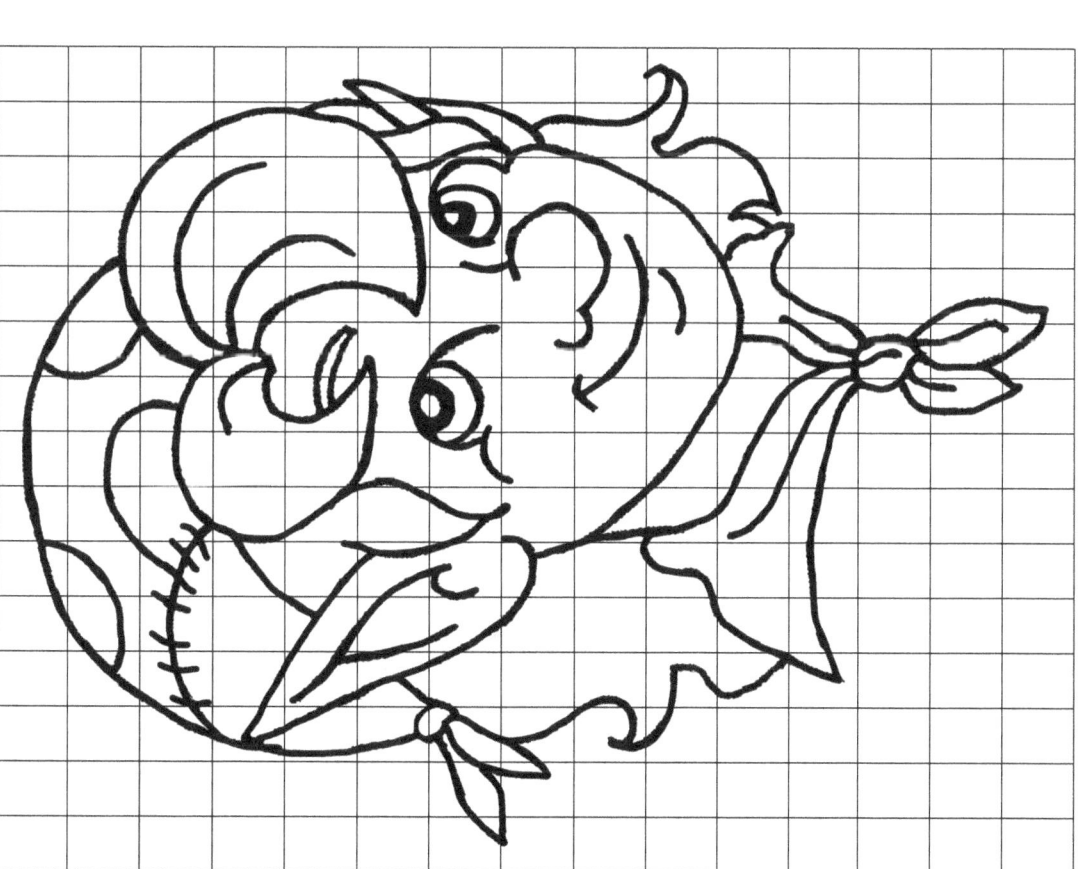

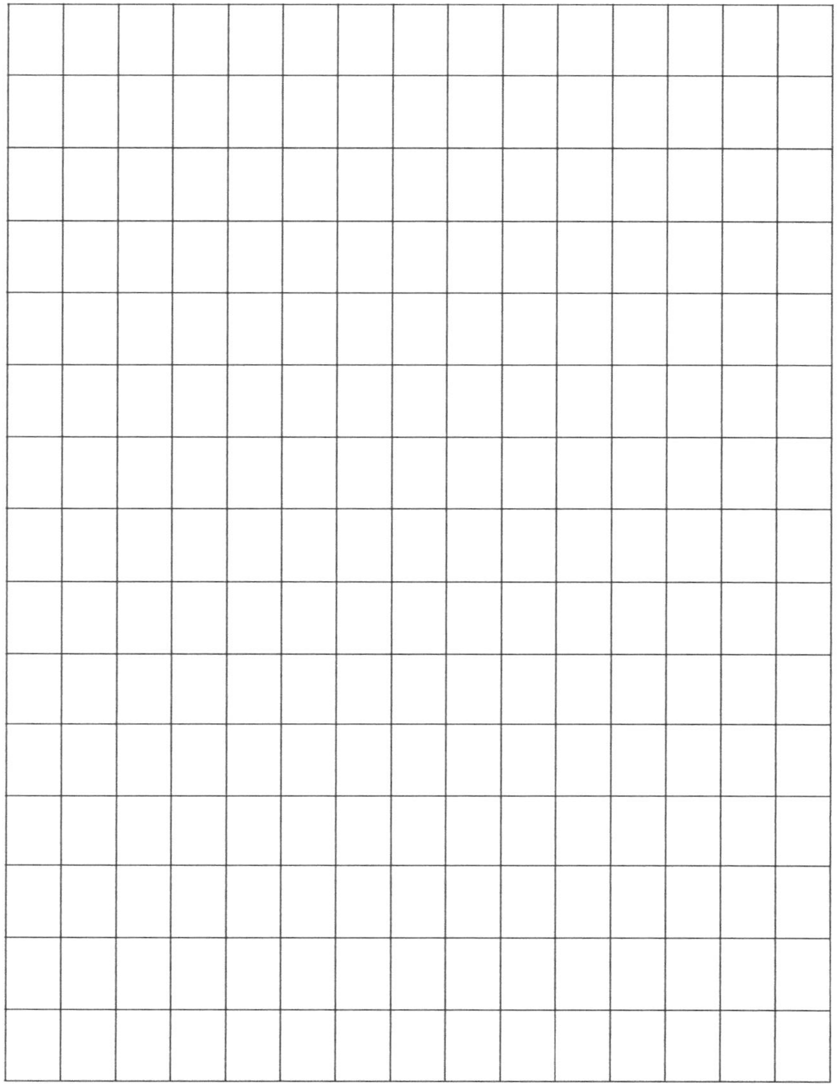

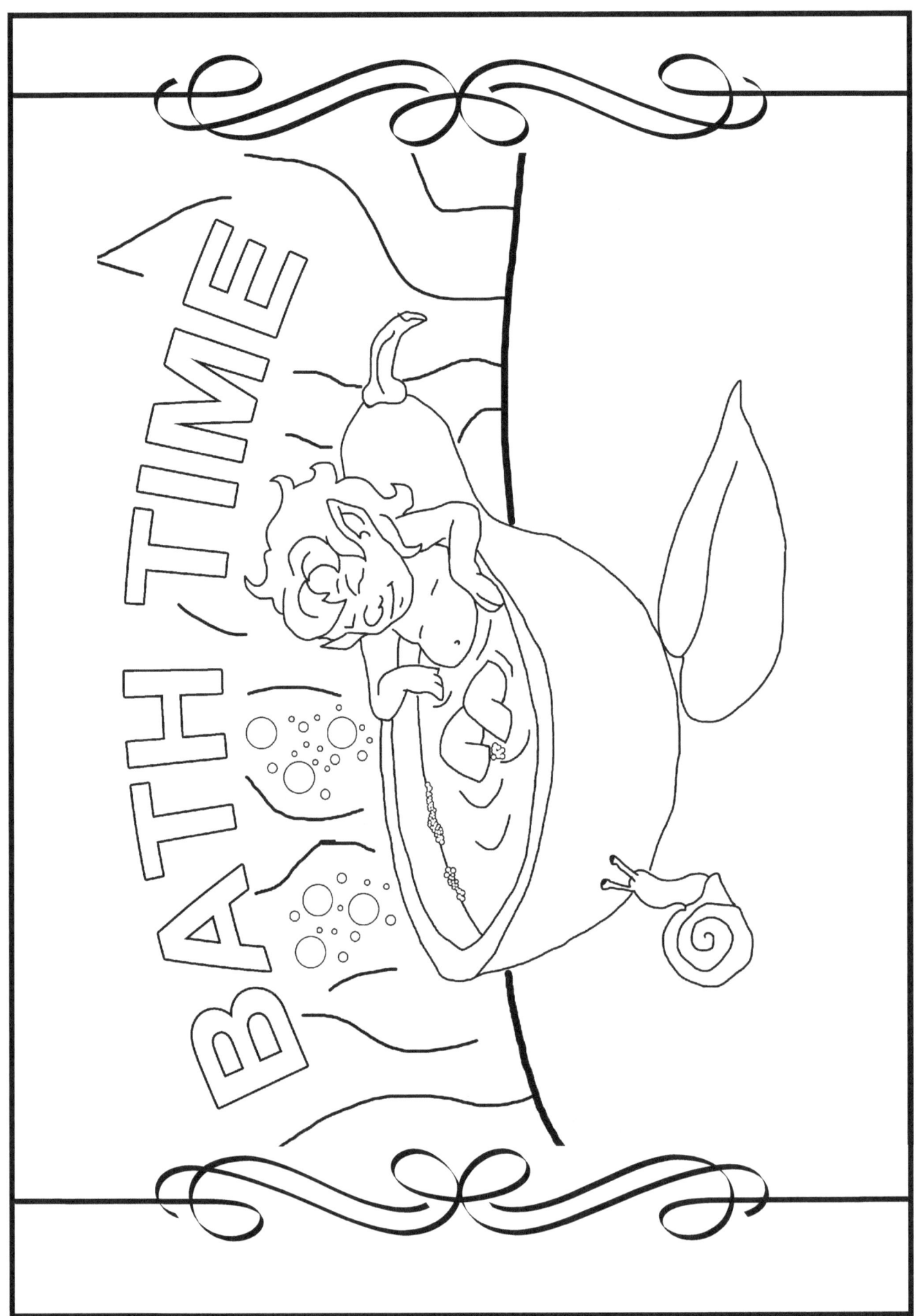

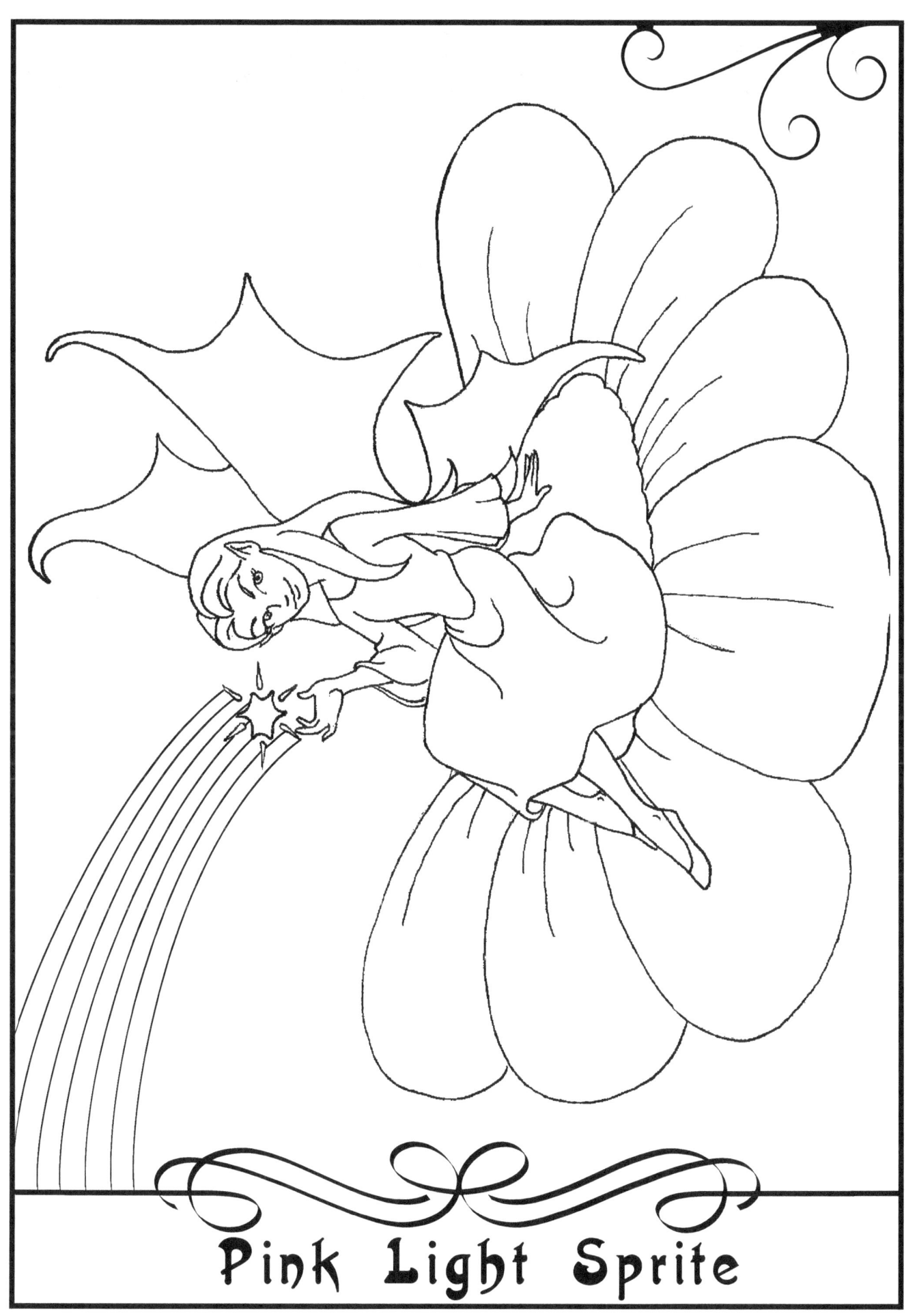

Pink Light Sprite

HIDDEN MESSAGE

Color only the letters with a ♥ to read a secret message from Hamilton Troll

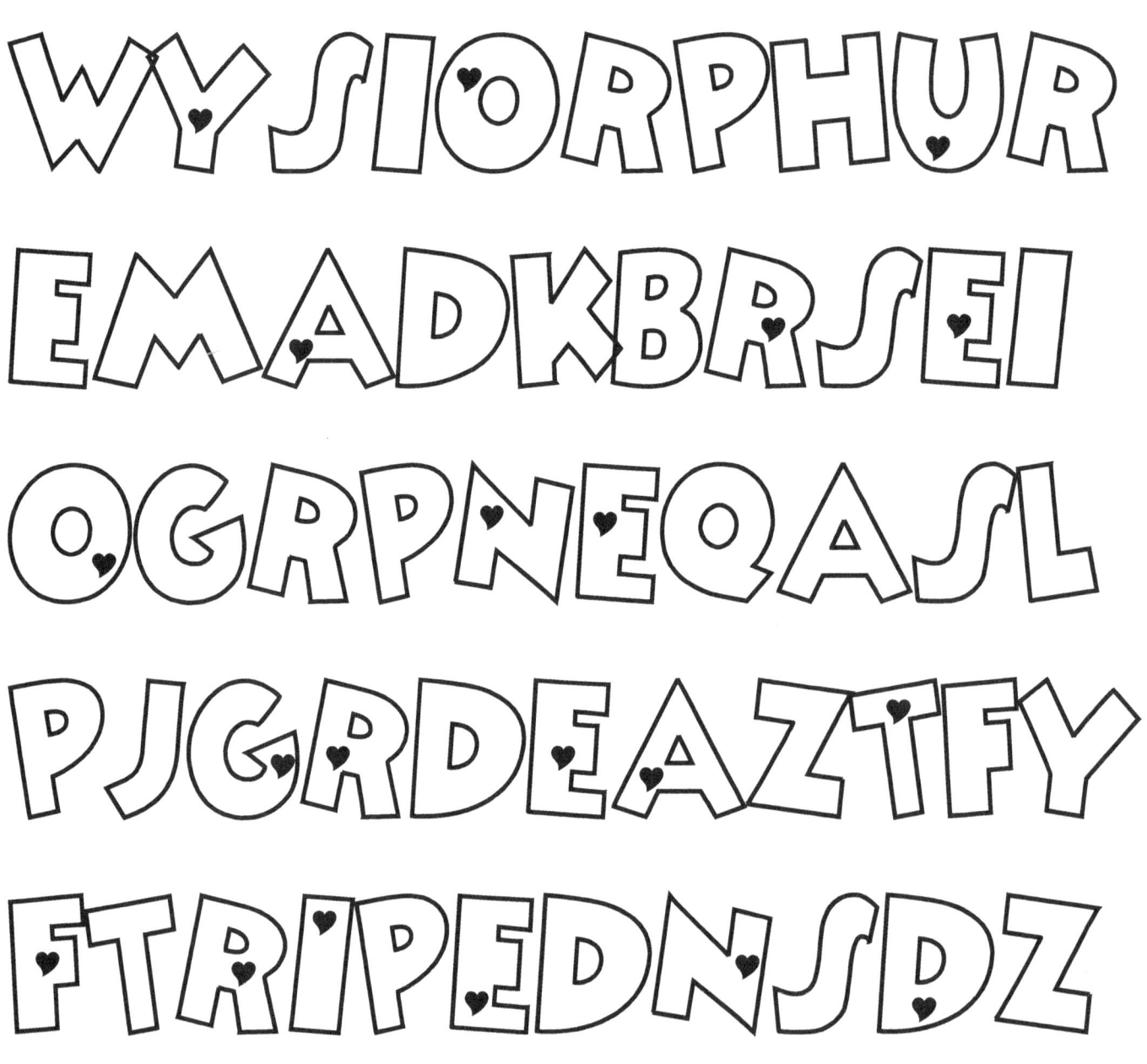

Write the message here:

YOU ARE ONE GREAT FRIEND

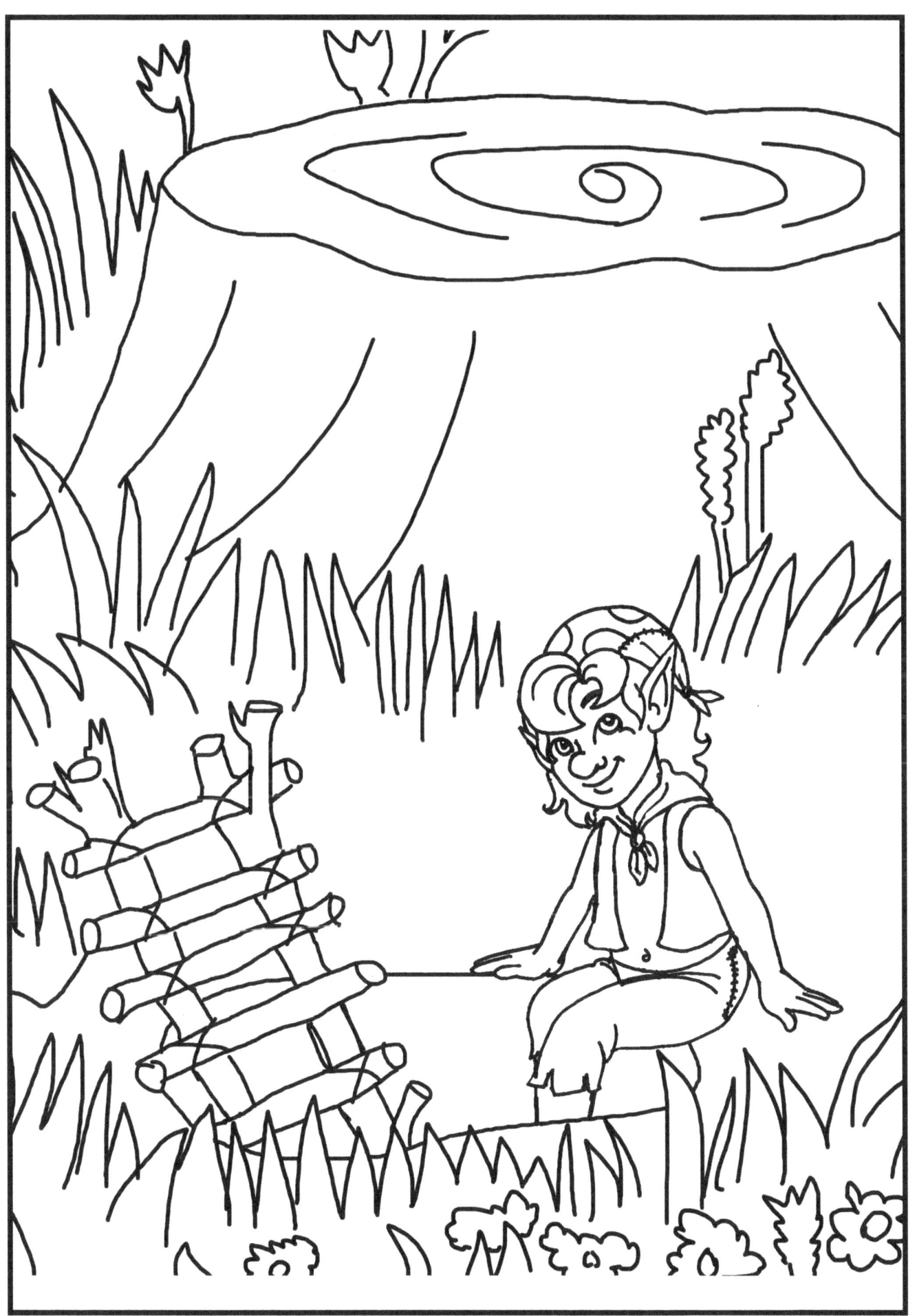

WORD SEARCH

S	Q	U	I	R	R	E	L	K	T
K	K	O	W	L	A	E	E	C	H
E	N	U	T	R	L	L	S	I	G
E	L	O	N	U	T	O	P	T	I
T	R	O	L	K	T	I	R	S	L
E	L	W	O	O	D	P	I	T	K
R	C	H	A	M	I	L	T	O	N
B	A	R	N	E	Y	B	E	E	I
R	E	K	A	T	I	H	W	O	P
C	H	A	T	T	E	R	T	O	N

HAMILTON	CHATTERTON
TROLL	SQUIRREL
PINK LIGHT	WHITAKER
SPRITE	OWL
SKEETER	ELWOOD
SKUNK	STICK
BARNEY BEE	NUT

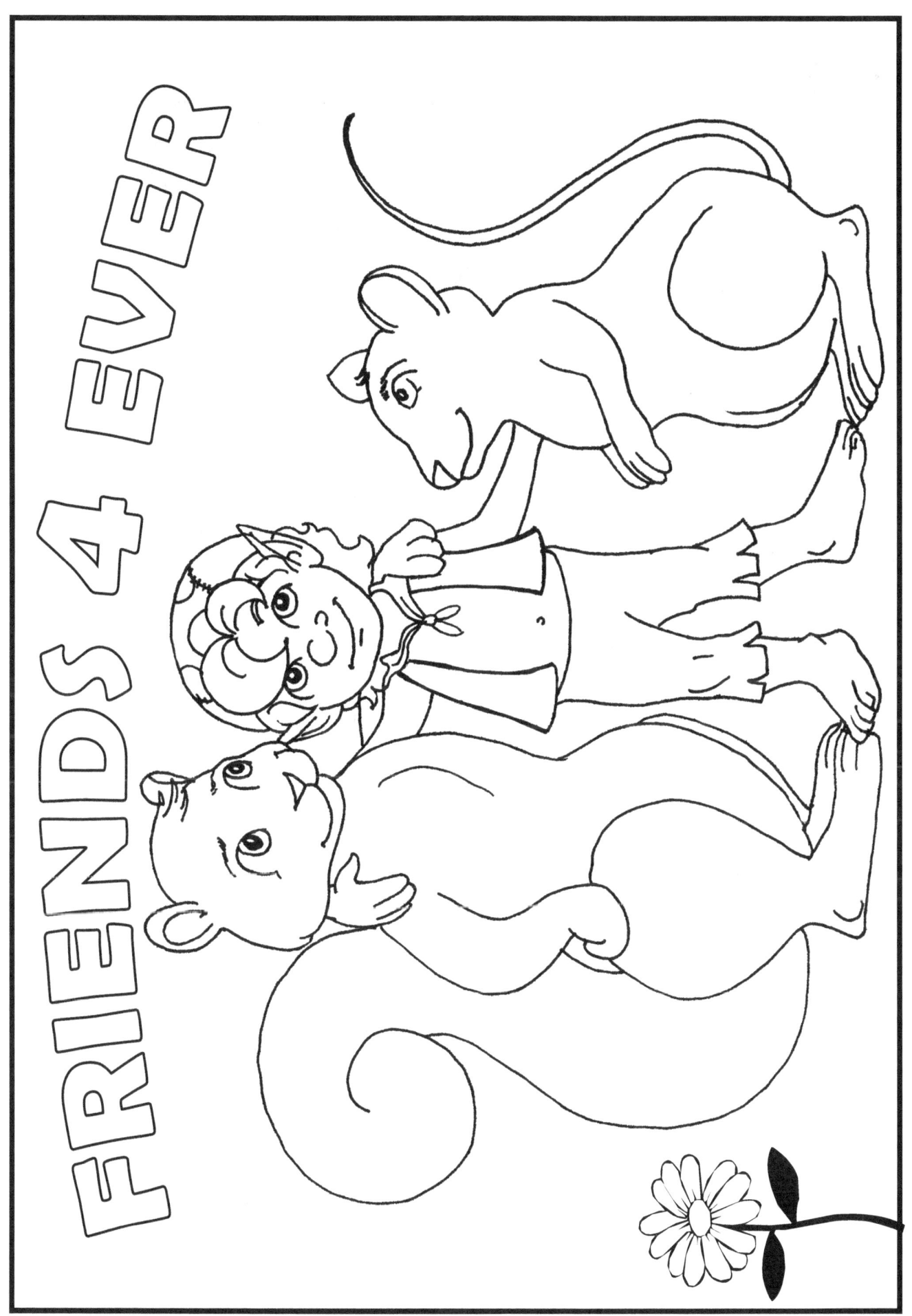

Starlit Troll

Starlit Troll is going to meet Hamilton Troll in book #11 of the 'meets' series. She is going to teach Hamilton that he can travel the world which will begin the 'visits' series in early 2016!

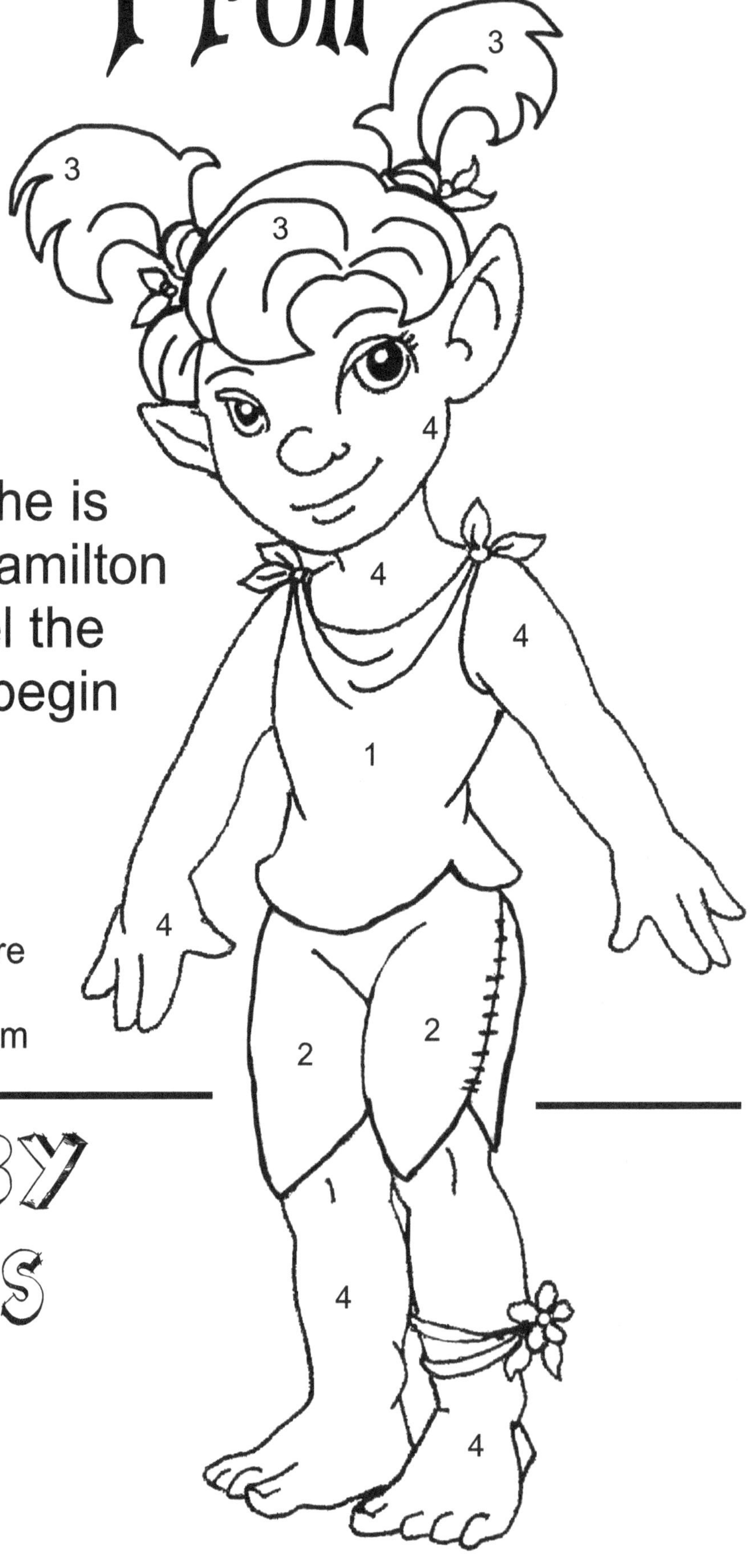

Keep up with the entire series online at www.HamiltonTroll.com

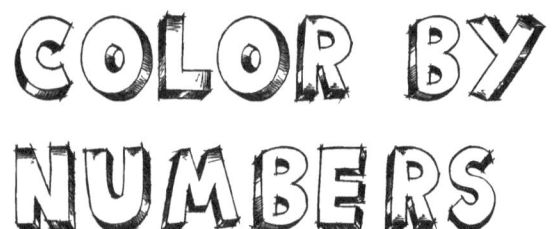

COLOR BY NUMBERS

1 Yellow
2 Brown
3 Dark Blue
4 Light Green

ANSWERS

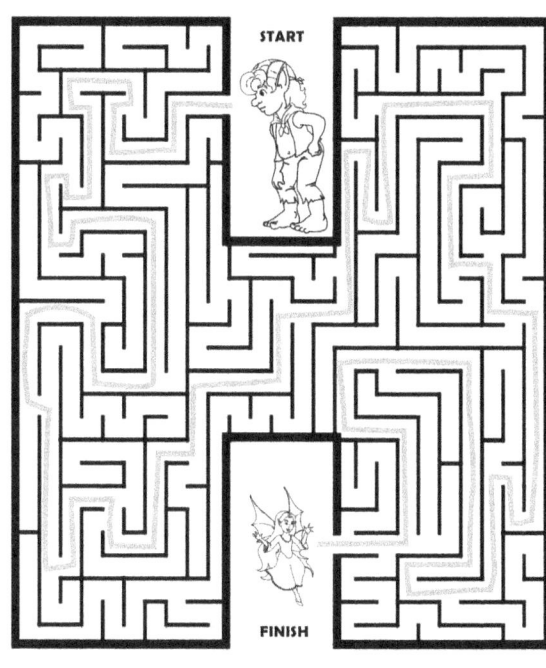

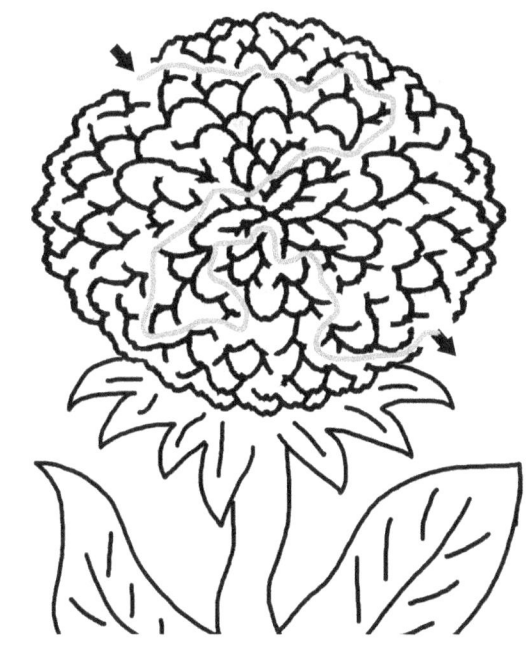

PINK LIGHT SPRITE
BARNEY BEE
AMARA ARMADILLO
WHITAKER OWL
MERLE MOUSE
ELWOOD
SKEETER SKUNK
HAMILTON TROLL
CHATTERTON

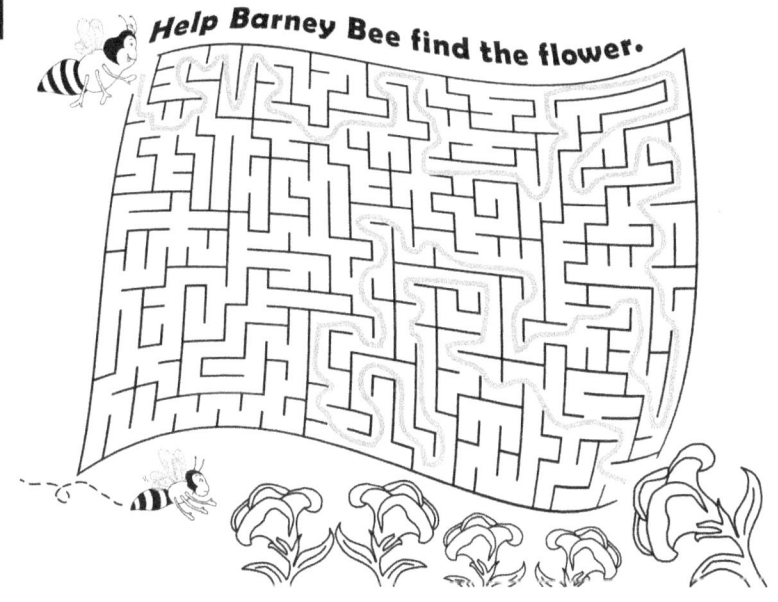

Help Barney Bee find the flower.

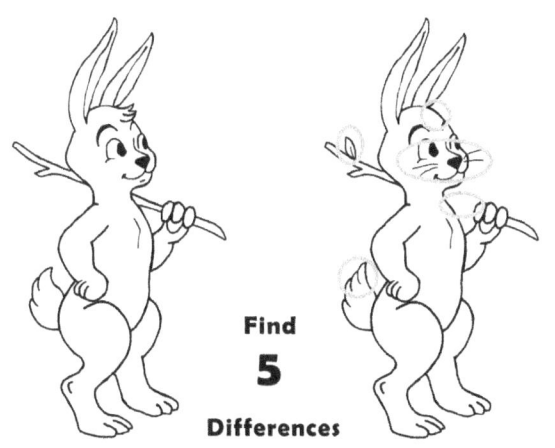

Find
5
Differences

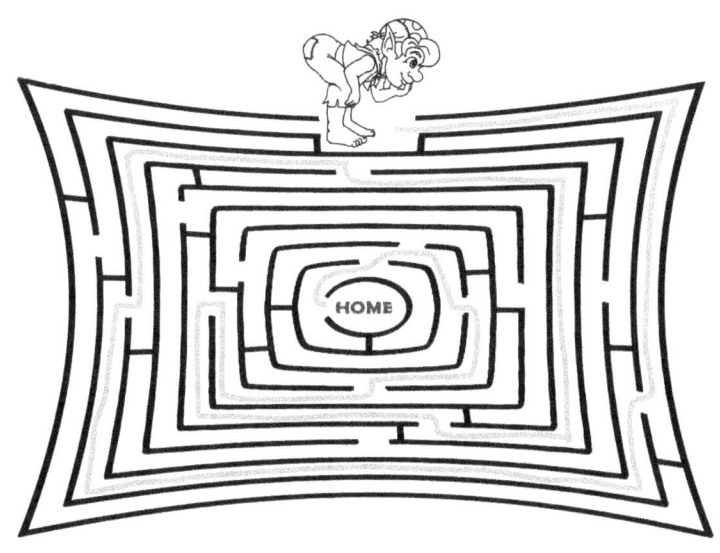

HOME

Which worm will Elwood get?

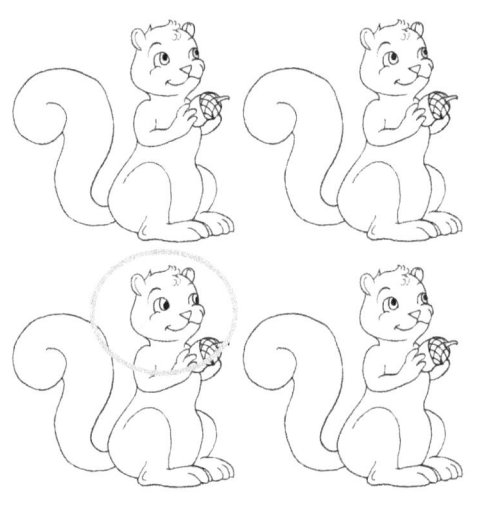

♥ YOU ARE ONE GREAT FRIEND

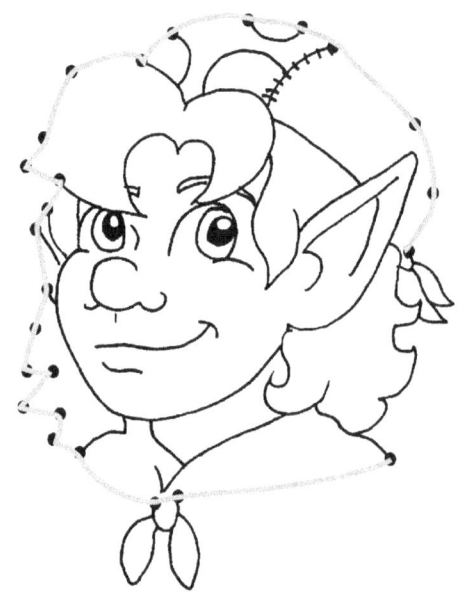

```
        D
    F L O P
        M
S
P O L L E N
R
I
S T I C K N U T
E           R
        H O O T   T
            R
            L
S Q U I R R E L
```

```
S Q U I R R E L K T
K K O W L A E E C H
E N U T R L I S I G
E L O N U T O P T I
T R O L K T I R S L
E L W O O D P I T K
R C H A M I L T O N
B A R N E Y B E E I
R E K A T I H W O P
C H A T T E R T O N
```

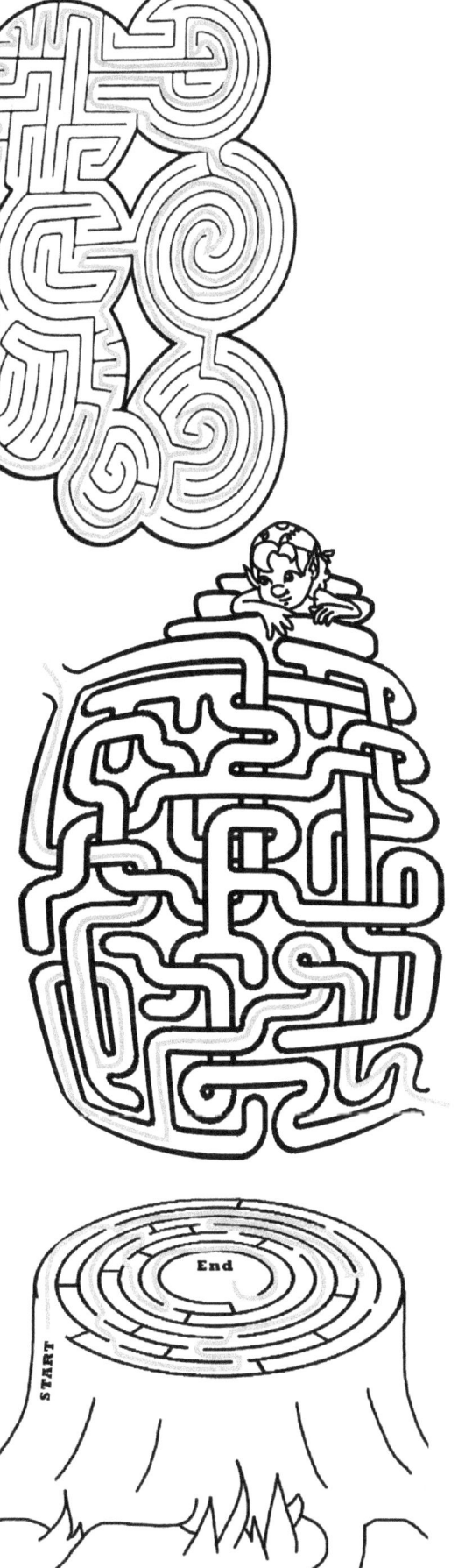

```
L I T O N O T L I M A H
H A H A M I L T O N O N
N A N H A M I N L O T A
O M M A H A M I L T O N
T I L I H T H A M L T N
L L O T L I M A H I T H
I I N I N T H A M M N A
M M M A H N O T I A O M
A A M I L T O N L H T I
H H O N O T L I M A L L
```

```
N A N O T R E C H A T N
C A T O O N C H A R O O
T H R E N C A R T T N T
R H E T R T O O R O C R
E R T R E H O E A N H E
T H T E T R T N H T A T
A T T A T T I H C E T A
H A A R A T R O N R T A
C R H H S H A T T R O H
T A C H A T E R T O N C
```

```
E I R T S P R I T E S
E S T S P R I T E S R
S S P R I T E S R S P
E T I R P S S P R F S
E I R T S P P S F S E
I S P R I E I S I T
T S P R T E T R T
S T E I R E P F
R P S S R R I E F
P R I T P T R I P S
S P R I T S P R I T E
P R I S P R I E T R
```

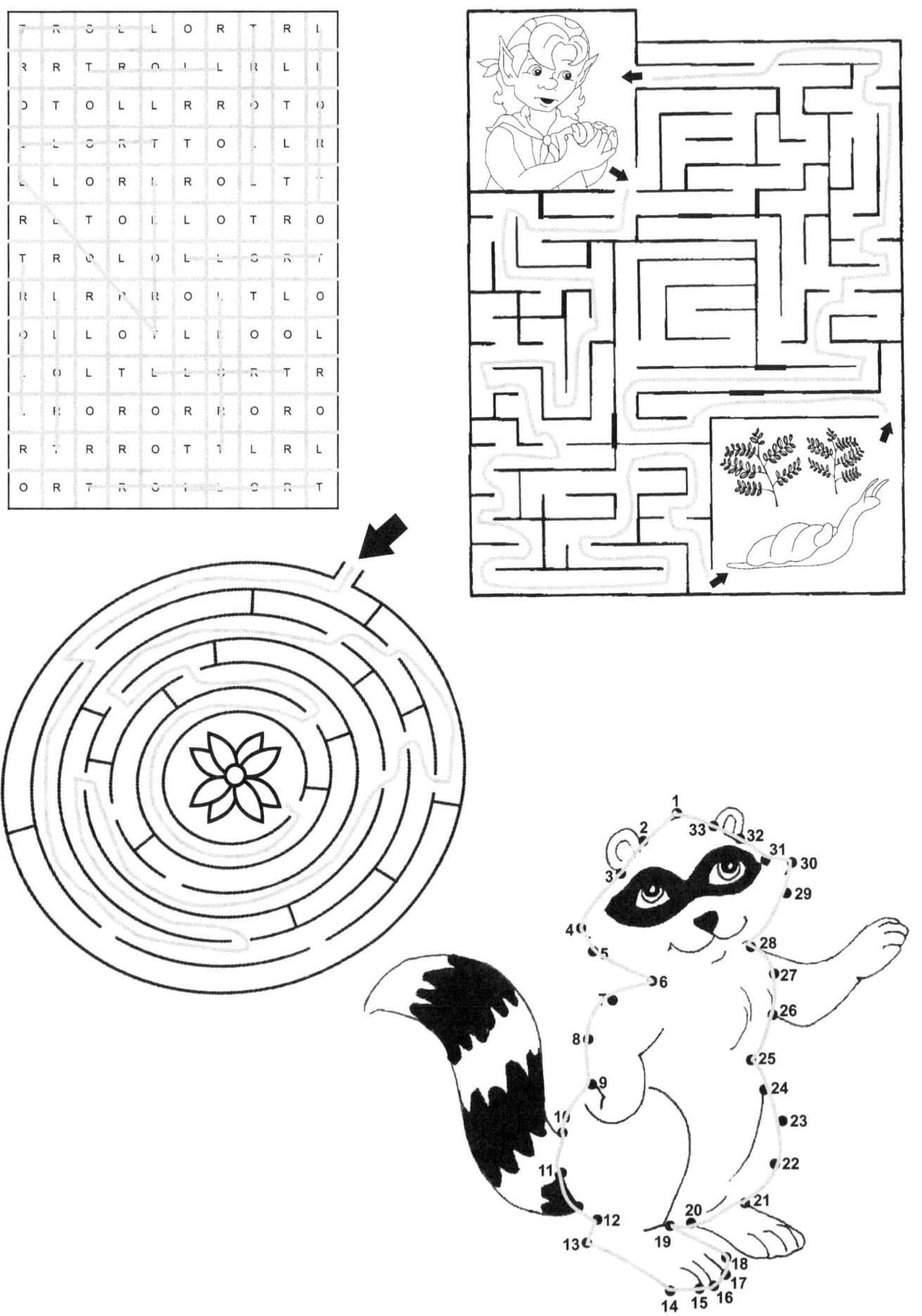

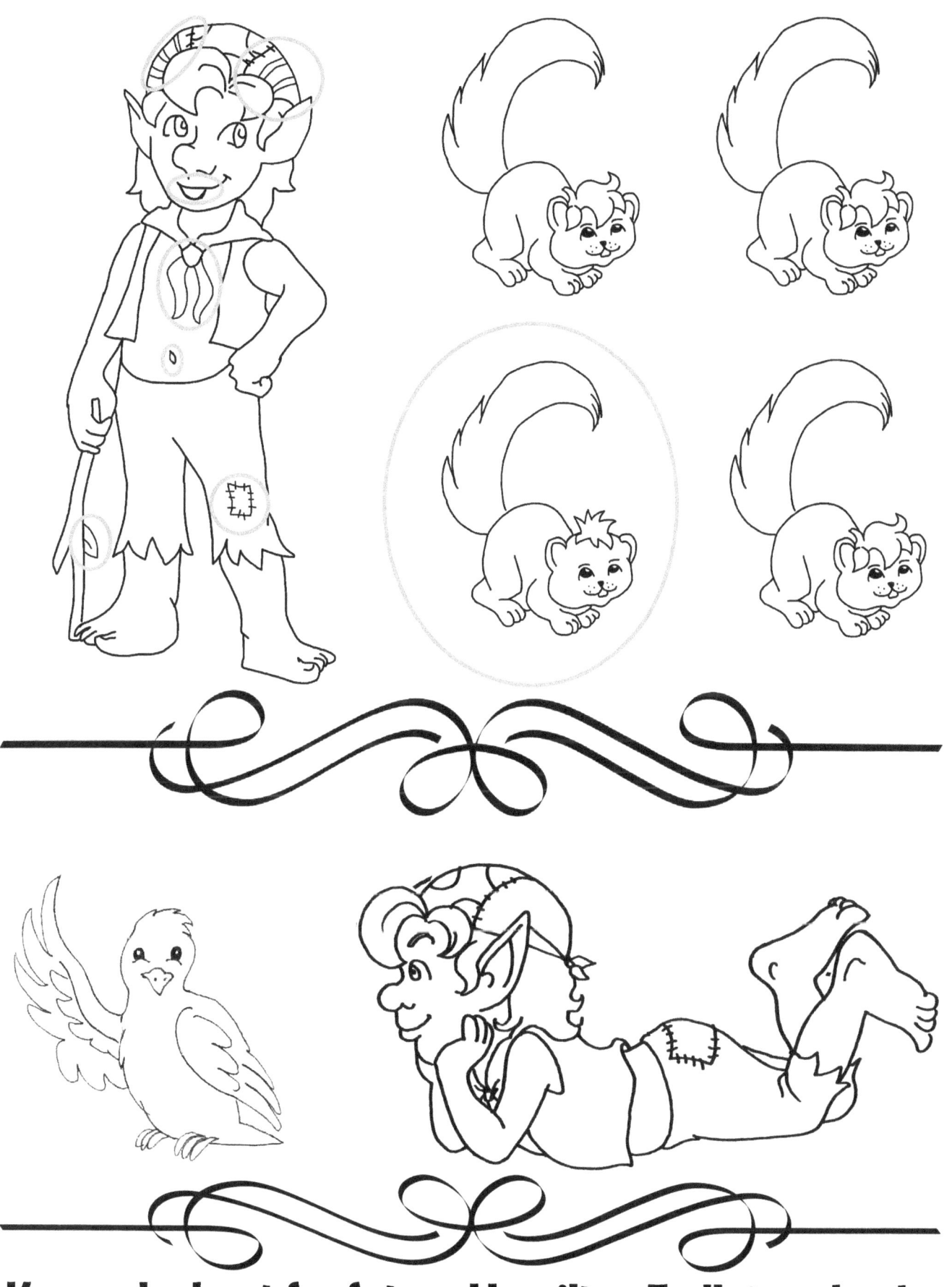

Keep a lookout for future Hamilton Troll story books and new coloring books. www.HamiltonTroll.com